THE DIVINITY OF CHRIST

By

Robert Hawker, D.D.

LATE VICAR OF CHARLES, PLYMOUTH

WIPF & STOCK · Eugene, Oregon

Wipf and Stock Publishers
199 W 8th Ave, Suite 3
Eugene, OR 97401

The Divinity of Christ
By Hawker, Robert
ISBN 13: 978-1-55635-702-2
ISBN 10: 1-55635-702-8
Publication date 11/8/2007
Previously published by Ebenezer Palmer, 1831

TO

THE RIGHT HONORABLE GEORGE MONTAGU,

LORD VISCOUNT MANDEVILLE, M. P.

COMMANDER IN THE ROYAL NAVY, &c. &c. &c.

WHOSE STEADFAST ATTACHMENT TO THE DOCTRINES OF THE REFORMATION, AND WHOSE LIBERALITY IN EXTENDING A KNOWLEDGE OF THEM;

WHOSE BENEVOLENCE IN AIDING AND PROTECTING THAT TOO LONG NEGLECTED CLASS OF MEN, DESTITUTE BRITISH SAILORS;

And whose General Devotedness

TO EVERY PLAN, WHICH HAS FOR ITS OBJECT THE AMELIORATION OF HUMAN MISERY, THE PREACHING OF A CRUCIFIED SAVIOUR, AND THE GLORY OF GOD AS THE ULTIMATE END OF ALL;

Shine so Conspicuously:

AND WHILE THEY RENDER HIS CHARACTER WORTHY OF GENERAL IMITATION WILL EMBALM HIS MEMORY IN THE HEARTS AND THE AFFECTIONS OF THE CHURCH OF CHRIST TO THE LATEST PERIOD OF TIME;

THIS EDITION

OF THE WRITINGS OF ONE OF THE BRIGHTEST ORNAMENTS OF OUR NATIONAL CHURCH, WHO WITH UNWEARIED ARDOUR CONSTANTLY AND FEARLESSLY EXHIBITED TO A PERISHING WORLD THE GLAD TIDINGS OF A FULL AND FREE SALVATION,

IS,

(WITH HIS LORDSHIP'S PERMISSION)

VERY RESPECTFULLY INSCRIBED

BY HIS LORDSHIP'S MOST OBEDIENT AND DEVOTED SERVANT,

THE PUBLISHER.

JUNE 30, 1831.

I am Dr Sir,
Yrs in the LORD,
Robert Hawker.

CONTENTS

PREFACE

TO THE PRESENT EDITION,

NOW FIRST PUBLISHED IN 1826.

The *Spiritual* Reader, conversant in divine things, will need no information to shew him, for whom these Sermons, on the Godhead of Christ were originally intended. He will perceive, that they were meant for such, as by regeneration had been brought into a capability, under divine teaching, of receiving "the things which are freely given to us of God," 1 Cor. ii. 12. But he will perceive also, that they were meant for such, as Paul calls "Babes in Christ," to be fed "with milk, and not with meat," 1 Cor. iii. 1, 2. Hence he will observe also, that the subject begins, and is carried on through the whole volume, more in a way of inquiry than decision: more with a view, that the Reader, matriculated in the school of Christ by the new birth, should form his *own* opinion, under divine teaching, than be led by the Writer's. And hence the question, with which the first sermon opens, is, in fact, carried on through every discourse that follows; and forms the conclusion for inquiry at the end—What think ye of Christ? And, the design herefrom is, as if personally addressed to every Reader; saying, You have now gone over some of the leading points of character, concerning the Almighty Author of salvation; the question from the whole now is, What think *you* of Christ?

Had these Sermons been originally designed for the higher taught classes, in the Church of CHRIST; the subject would have been treated, in a much greater extent, in the mysteries of the gospel; and in the inquiry concerning Him, "whom to know is life eternal;" here it would have been prosecuted, under all its bearings. The glorious doctrine of the most holy Trinity would have been the basis (as it is in itself of all revelation) of these Sermons, and every view of our most glorious CHRIST would have been taken from this standard. Wherefore this was not then done, hath been assigned; and the motive, if wrong, must be its apology. But now, after a lapse of time, of *six and thirty years*; spared by the Lord to the present period; and called upon for a new edition of this work; in revising the whole, and to render the whole, under sovereign grace, more generally useful to the church at large; I have judged it right to begin where GOD himself in his gracious revelations of himself to his church began; and take our *datum* in proof of the GODHEAD of CHRIST, from the doctrine of "the Holy Three which bear record in heaven: for these Three are One," 1 John v. 7. This foundation, spiritually and scripturally formed in the mind by an unction from the LORD, (1 John ii. 20.) will prepare the enlightened believer to a proper apprehension of his Almighty Person, who in his divine essence and nature is one of those Holy Three, constituting GODHEAD; and who, by the assumption of our nature hath come forth to make a revelation of the purpose, counsel, will, and pleasure of JEHOVAH in his Trinity of Persons; and is the great medium of all communication, and the visible JEHOVAH to the church, in all the departments of nature, providence, grace, and glory.

Every part and portion of the word of GOD tends to proclaim the unity of the Divine Essence, in his Trinity of Persons. But as if, in greater condescension still, the LORD JEHOVAH not only proclaims this foundation truth; but proceeds to give full and repeated testimonies of the same. For while we hear JEHOVAH call himself "the High and Lofty One that inhabiteth eternity, whose name is Holy," (Isaiah lvii. 15.) and by his servant the prophet saith, "Hear, O Israel! the LORD our GOD is one LORD!" (Deut. vi. 4.) he no less teacheth the church, that his nature, and being, and essence, differs from all the creatures he hath called into existence; for it is in a Trinity of Persons. Hence we find the sacred Three speaking *to* each other, and speaking *of* each other; and in a way, and manner, as decidedly define a distinction of Persons, while constituting One, and the same eternal essence of GODHEAD. I stay not to quote the many passages to this amount, in both Testaments of Scripture; for this would form a Treatise of itself, more than a Preface. But I refer you to some few in point: Ps. cx. 1; xlv. 6, 7; xl. 6; with Heb. x. 5. John's Gospel in every part. Acts xiii, 1, 2, &c.

But what is very highly observable, and if the Reader hath not already been acquainted with it, and is a follower of CHRIST in the regeneration, he will find an high gratification from, is, that the conferences of the Holy Three in One with each other, as recorded in the Bible, are chiefly, if not altogether, concerning the church. This is a wonderful condescension in the High and Lofty One inhabiting eternity, and ought to be everlastingly uppermost in our hearts. It begins at the very first chapter of sacred Scripture, Gen. i. 26. where we find the sacred language: "Let us make man in our image, after our likeness." Again, "Let us go down and there confound their language," Gen. xi. 7. And this (which is but little considered) was more in mercy than judgment; for it laid the foundation for the miraculous gift of tongues, at the day of Pentecost, Acts ii. 4. We have another beautiful illustration of this distinction of Persons in the GODHEAD, conversing about the church, in the several acts of grace towards the church, as related in the vision of Isaiah, sixth chapter, and explained Acts xxviii. 26.

But we must not stop here; for blessed be our God, in his Trinity of Persons, he hath not stopped here. Acts of unparalleled grace are unfolded, of this distinction of Persons in the GODHEAD, and as particularly made known to the church in the several manifestations of love from each, and to every individual of CHRIST's mystical body. It is the FATHER, by whom the whole family the church, is named, in heaven and in earth, Ephes. iii. 14. His is the choice of their persons; his, the adoption of them as children; his, the acceptation of them in CHRIST, Ephes. i. 4—6. It is GOD the SON, who hath espoused them to himself; taken their nature, and redeemed them from the Adam-fall transgression "by the sacrifice of himself," Isa. liv. 5. Hosea ii. 19. Heb. ii. 16, &c. It is GOD the HOLY GHOST, who hath anointed them together with CHRIST; and by his own personal work, carries on the whole process in the renewal of our nature, from the fall, from grace to glory, Titus iii. 4, 5, 6. Now these, and the like views (and which the reader will not fail, I hope, to observe, are all founded on scripture authority) will not only prepare the regenerated child of GOD, for receiving the testimonies selected in this volume of the GODHEAD of CHRIST: but, under a divine unction from the LORD, will tend to open the finer feelings of the soul, to the spiritual enjoyment of those distinct acts of the FATHER, SON, and HOLY GHOST, and induce what is the highest proof of being a partaker of grace; namely, a corresponding affection of love, adoration, and praise to the united Author of such unspeakable mercies.

I am led to hope, that the revision of this Work in this manner, for the present edition, will, under the LORD's blessing tend to render it more useful. Even the more advanced believer in the church of GOD, by beginning with the doctrine of the Holy Trinity, will find the advantage in contemplating the vast assemblage of scripture proofs here brought into one view, of the GODHEAD of CHRIST. And our little children in the divine life, will be led to trace up the glorious subject, of CHRIST'S GODHEAD, to behold his oneness in the unity of the divine essence, and Trinity of Persons according to our LORD'S own statement: "If ye had known me, ye should have known my Father also. He that hath seen me, hath seen my Father also!" John xiv. 7, 9.

The reader of the former editions will observe that I have omitted in this all reference to Socinian writers. Indeed, I thought it *then*, but am more convinced *now*, it was labour lost. For while the Holy Scripture asserts, that "the natural man cannot receive the things of the SPIRIT of GOD," (1 Cor. ii. 14.) to what purpose appeal to them? Add to this weighty consideration, the writings of such men are ephemeral, and the sooner they are consigned to their just oblivion the better. But in the place of such quotations, I have endeavoured to raise up, here and there, through the body of the Work, spiritual reflections, which I hope the LORD will make profitable to Spiritual Readers.

I cannot close my Preface without pausing to observe, and in that observation, to adore, distinguishing grace, for preserving a life so marked with evil, (Ps. xxxvi. 1.) through a period of *six and thirty years;* and for enabling me to revise these early labours. "LORD! what am I! and what is my father's house?"—The GOD of our LORD JESUS CHRIST, the FATHER of glory, give (if it be His blessed will) to every redeemed and regenerated Reader, that his grace may incline to the perusal of these Sermons, "the spirit of wisdom and revelation in the knowledge of Him; the eyes of their understanding being enlightened, that they may know what is the hope of his calling, and what the riches of the glory of his inheritance in the saints; and what is the exceeding greatness of his power to us-ward who believe!" And through rich, free, full, sovereign grace, they may "be able to comprehend with all saints, what is the breadth, and length, and depth, and height; and to know the love of CHRIST, which passeth knowledge, that we may be filled with all the fulness of GOD!"

PLYMOUTH, CHARLES' VICARAGE,
April 13, 1826.

THE

ORIGINAL PREFACE

TO THE FIRST EDITION,

PUBLISHED IN 1790—1.

It may be expected that some reason should be assigned for publishing the following Sermons, upon a subject which hath already received so much discussion. And indeed, were the merits of the performance the only recommendation, it is more than probable the work itself would never have been brought forth to public view. But this, however, is the smallest consideration for its appearance.

The Sermons were composed for the particular edification of those persons in whose spiritual concerns the Author considers himself highly interested, and who are justly entitled to his best and most diligent labours. And his sole object was to prevent the minds of his congregation from being led away from what he humbly conceives to be the pure faith of the Gospel, by the revival of an opinion long since exploded, but which seems to be mingling with the fashionable doctrines of the present day.

As this purpose might have been sufficiently answered from the pulpit, the Author would have rested satisfied with the consciousness of having discharged by that means his duty, and with having given his public testimony, however trifling, to the important cause. But when he found the sincerity of the Established Clergy called in question; and it was confidently said, that but few of them believed the doctrines they professed, he concluded that he ought not to confine his sentiments within the narrow limits of his own parish, but declare himself in a more public way, to be one of those *supposed* few, whose profession and convictions are happily blended.

Although he hath said this, in order to account for the publication of the following Sermons, he has not said it with a view to deprecate the severity of criticism, or to effect popularity. To assert the dignity of our most glorious God and Saviour, the great founder of the Gospel, is the indispensable duty of every faithful servant of Jesus, whatever inconveniences he may suffer in so just a cause. And God forbid that any man who bears this character, should recede from any apprehension in speaking of *his* divinity upon *earth* through whom alone, in his incommunicable salvation, our everlasting happiness is secured *in heaven*. If he shrinks with fear from what may be the result of this publication, it is not from the dread of criticism (the shafts of which, upon the present occasion, must lose their power to wound,) but his fear is, lest the cause he wishes to support, should suffer from the very imperfect manner in which he had treated it.

He hath only further to request, that the candid reader will make all proper allowances for the great length into which he has been unavoidably carried, in the induction of particulars towards the accomplishment of the end intended. Did he write for the amusement of a light hour, he could not hope, that a subject in which there is so little variety, and such great sameness of argument, would procure many readers. But as the design is of a different nature, he trusts the infinite importance of it will be a sufficient apology with those who read from better motives.

Whilst he writes, his eyes are to the Lord that a divine blessing may attend the serious perusal; and if these Discourses be found to contain any thing of a salutary tendency, either to confirm the faith of the believer, or to guide the uninformed in his pursuit of truth; that God "in all things be glorified, through Jesus Christ."

SERMON I.

MATTHEW xxii. 42.

What think ye of Christ? whose Son is he?

THE religion of Jesus which we profess, demands our attention by every argument capable of interesting the human heart. The manner of its first introduction, the immense preparation which, through so many ages, preceded its establishment, its descent to us, sealed with the blood of apostles and martyrs, nay, even "God himself confirming the word with signs and wonders, and gifts of the Holy Ghost," (Heb. ii. 4.) are circumstances so very striking, as seem to render it impossible for any man to suppose, that all this mighty apparatus was intended to refer to a matter, trifling in its nature, and of no material consequence whether neglected or despised. "If they escaped not who refused him that spake on earth, much more shall not we escape, if we turn away from him that speaketh from heaven," (Heb. xii. 25.)

But while we feel the full influence, and great importance of the gospel, we cannot but be proportionably anxious to know the truth as it is in Jesus: that we may embrace "that faith," and *that faith only*, "which was once delivered unto the saints," (Jude 3.) For, however pure the fountain from whence the word of God first issued, yet if it comes to us through tainted and corrupt channels, how shall we be assured that it hath not imbibed a portion of impurity?

It is a well-known truth, and cannot be dissembled, that, from the very infancy of Christianity, errors crept into the church. The tares of infidelity and scepticism were early sown with the good seed. They sprung up and appeared together, and both (as our blessed Lord himself predicted) "will grow together unto the harvest," (Matt. xiii. 30.) But let not the faithful despond on this account. Tares are always to be discerned from good seed. The LORD in his providence hath a gracious design in every dispensation. "There must be heresies among you," (saith an apostle) "that they which are approved may be made manifest among you," (1 Cor. xi. 19.) Even the errors of opinion, therefore, are not without their use in the present state of discipline, for they serve to ascertain and prove the truth. And from this ordeal the gospel hath been always found to come forth, not only with more clearness, but also bringing with it increasing evidence of its divine authority.

Every age hath been distinguished by some peculiar mode of hostility against the principles of our holy faith. By open attack, and by insidious design, the false friend and the professed foe have alike aimed their blows, to effect the ruin of the church. But we know who it is that hath said, his "church is founded on a rock, against which the gates of hell shall not prevail," (Matt. xvi. 18.) The enemies who have come forward against Christianity, have only broken their arrows against its impenetrable shield, and, tired of the unequal combat, have withdrawn from the field in sullen silence.

It would, however, be in vain to expect that all opposition should cease. The LORD the SPIRIT permits the existence of error, with a view to accomplish some greater good. By this means the truth, when discovered, is placed on a more firm and sure foundation, and in the mean time it answers the necessary ends of trial to exercise the faith of the true believer.

Besides, while the corrupt passions of the human mind remain unreformed, there will be always some who will find an interest in opposing the pure system of morality contained in the gospel, and while religion is sought for by others, "through philosophy and vain deceit, after the tradition of men, and not after Christ," (Coloss. ii. 8.), the pride of reason will not easily bend to the hunbleness and docility of little children, which is so necessary to the reception of those doctrines by which the Christian faith is peculiarly known. From both these causes, therefore, the religion of Jesus will be always sure to meet with opposition.

The controversy of the present hour seems to be particularly of this latter kind. Under the specious pretence that reason alone is competent to determine the measure of religious faith, a certain class of men (and in the garb of friends to Christianity too) have presumed to analyze the several parts of revelation by this standard, and have peremptorily rejected every thing beyond the power of reason to account for, as impossible to have proceeded from God. Thus, with a rash and bold hand, they have torn from the gospel all the sacred mysteries of our holy faith, reduced the whole to a mere system of ethics, and degraded the divine Author of our salvation to a character no higher than that of a moral teacher—the equal of Socrates or Confucius. Nay, to such an height hath this doctrine advanced, that he who hath the dangerous honour of pre-eminence in this opinion hath declared, that the sentiments even of an apostle are invalid, and of no weight with him.*

When errors of this fatal tendency spring up in the world, and come forth to the public under the sanction of distinguished names, we cannot be too much upon our guard, to repel the seducing influence. The GODHEAD of CHRIST is the chief corner-stone in the edifice

* Dr. Priestley.

of Christianity. Remove this from the building and the whole fabric immediately totters. The foundation is shaken to the very centre. There appears at once an evident disproportion between the end and the means; the importance of the object proposed, and the person by whom it was accomplished. And then the great doctrine of atonement falls to the ground, and all the rich promises of the gospel are done away.

In matters of less moment, though we cannot but lament that there should be any dissensions amongst sincere professors of Christianity, yet when these refer to points of mere form or ceremony, and concern not the fundamentals of religion, it were a folly to contend. They arise from the weaknesses and prejudices of human nature, and are the result of that imperfection and frailty, which mark our very best performances. But when so vital a part of the gospel is attacked; the divinity of our blessed Lord palpably denied; himself classed among fallible men; all adoration to him expressly forbidden; and the members of the established Church branded with idolatry: it is impossible to regard such reproaches with indifference. How can any true believer hear, with unconcern, that blessed Person, by whose sacred name we are called, thus degraded and traduced? Surely it must be a duty to come forward, and with becoming confidence assert the dignity of that God under whose banner we serve, and the purity of that form of worship which we profess! Against assaults of this nature it can be no bigotry to remonstrate; nor will the just defence of our principles be deemed, by any liberal mind, an ill-timed zeal. Nay, our silence might rather be construed into a tacit acknowledgment that we thought the charge unanswerable, and therefore meanly took refuge under an establishment which we were unable to defend.

But though gratitude, duty, and all the important

interests of religion, demand this from us, and to remain supine and indifferent would be unpardonably criminal, yet, in opposing the *opinions*, we never oppose the *persons* of men. "The weapons of our warfare are not carnal, but mighty through God, to the pulling down of strong holds, and bringing into captivity every thought to the obedience of Christ," (2 Cor. x. 4, 5.) In the investigation of truth, every sincere friend to the gospel must wish, that all enquiries may be pursued, not only with Christian temper and candour, but with somewhat more than these, with affection and goodwill. It is not for the triumph of opinion we contend, but for truth. Our most earnest desires are, that "all may came to the knowledge of the truth and be saved," (1 Tim. ii. 4.) While anxious therefore, in the pursuit of this great point, we condemn no man for his religious principles. "To his own master he standeth or falleth," (Rom. xiv. 4.) Too conscious of our own manifold imperfections, we dare not be rigorous and unmerciful to the imperfections of others. And surrounded as we are with so much darkness in the present state of being, that we can hardly judge of the objects which are near us with any precision or certainty, we are well aware how little the wisest of us know of the nature and dispensations of God. It were to be wished that all parties and persuasions of Christians would duly consider this circumstance, that every one might "learn to think humbly of himself, and as he ought to think." But what a comfortable and encouraging relief to the mind is that gracious promise of scripture; that if we are brought under the blessed direction of the great Spirit of truth, "he will guide us into all truth," (John xiv. 13.) "If we trust in the Lord, and lean not upon our own understanding, but in all our ways acknowledgé him, he will direct our paths," (Prov. iii. 5, 6.) For "the secret of the Lord is with them that fear him, and he will shew them his covenant," (Ps. xxv. 13.)

With these objects in view, and under an humble hope of divine assistance, it is my intention, in this and a few following discourses, to examine the evidences of our Lord's divinity. The question is exceedingly interesting, and the event important. For if it can be proved that the testimony of scripture is against this doctrine; it will follow, that the faith we profess, and the form of worship we observe, are founded on wrong principles; and all the venerable sanction of names, or the zeal of godly reformers, will be utterly insufficient to justify our continuance in them. But should it appear from the strictest investigation, that this great article of our church arises immediately from the scriptures themselves, and derives its influence wholly from this supreme authority; we have only to pity and pray for the conversion of those who differ from us. Their objections, instead of injuring our cause, will have proved beneficial to it, by enabling us to shew that "our faith does not stand in the wisdom of men, but in the power of God," (1 Cor. ii. 5.)

In the prosecution of this design, it will be my duty to bring before you the evidences we are in possession of, to prove the GODHEAD of CHRIST. It will be yours to examine the same with carefulness and impartiality. And as our salvation is blended together, and rests upon the same common cause, you will give credit at least to my integrity, if not to my understanding. I should be utterly unworthy the sacred office I hold among you, were I capable of temporizing upon so awful a concern. I scruple not therefore to say, I have received myself the belief of this great doctrine with the fullest conviction. It is the faith in which I trust, under the divine grace, always to live, and in which

I hope to die. But, while anxious to discharge what appears to be only my duty, in placing this great principle of the gospel before you, upon its proper basis, I desire no one implicitly to follow my opinion. Upon so momentous a concern, every man, as far as he is able, should judge for himself. Like the Bereans, who are mentioned in sacred history with such honourable testimony, I would wish you to "search the scriptures daily whether these things are so," (Acts xvii. 11.) Happy is that Christian whose experience in divine truths confirms the doctrines there revealed! Who (as the apostle says) from "believing on the Son of God hath the witness in himself," (1 John v. 10.) If religion be at all important, it must be highly important; indifference is unpardonable; inattention somewhat worse than folly. It is certainly the duty of every individual to be able to satisfy his own mind at least, if not to give an answer to others, of the hope that is in him: and that man must be strangely lost to all the great objects of eternity, who can sit down regardless in a matter of such infinite consequence, and which so highly concerns the salvation of his soul. Bend with me, I beseech you, before the awful throne of God, and let us humbly implore assistance from above, that the attention to this solemn subject, both of Him who speaks and those who hear, may be rewarded with his grace. That "God may give unto us the spirit of wisdom and revelation in the knowledge of him: the eyes of our understanding being enlightened, that we may know what is the hope of our calling, (Eph. i. 18, 19,) that we may prove things that are excellent, and that we may be sincere and without offence unto the day of Christ," (Phil. i. 10.)

And here, before I open the evidences in support of our blessed Lord's divinity, I beg once for all to premise, that I shall draw no conclusions in favour of this doctrine, but from Scripture; for on all disputable points in religion, this certainly is the only unerring standard of our judgment. I am free to confess that the whole body of commentators are nothing decisive with me on this important point. Whoever implicitly follows the opinions of men may be deceived. From the pure and uncorrupt word of God, there can be no danger of error or delusion. It is to this authority only I bend: and I trust you will find nothing in the course of these sermons insisted upon with the smallest emphasis, but what can clearly be proved from the testimony of Scripture.*

It will be unnecessary to produce any evidence of the authenticity of the sacred books themselves. The hardiest champions of fidelity have never yet been able to disprove the marks of genuine truth and purity with which these records are transmitted to us. Were these discourses, indeed, levelled against the controversial writings of deists, it might be needful to take a larger circuit, and

* I take occasion thus early in the prosecution of the work to observe to the Reader, that in this Edition, I have totally omitted speaking of the gracious acts of JEHOVAH, in his Trinity of Persons towards his people, as was injudiciously done in the former Editions under the term of *Office*. I know it is much used by many well-taught souls of the LORD's people: and I fell into the same error. But, according to my present views, I consider the term highly unsuitable and degrading: yea, somewhat worse than both. JEHOVAH hath indeed, in his Trinity of Persons, graciously condescended, to guarantee to his Church in CHRIST, an assurance, that each glorious Person in the GODHEAD, in the economy and covenant of grace, will fulfil all "the good pleasure of his will," and confirm all his promises in CHRIST. But while GOD our FATHER hath engaged in all these blissful things as our FATHER, shall we call this fatherly love an *office?* Is that unparalleled instance of love in One of the Persons taking into union with him our nature, an *office?* And all the rich comforts and consolations of the Holy Ghost, so many *offices?* We do not do so in the common charities and relations of life. My father in nature is not my father in *office*, but in *reality:* and by that tie we are brought into a very sweet and endearing relationship. How infinitely more in those spiritual and eternal connexions into which the Church is brought by our adoption as children in CHRIST! John would not have called such acts of grace acts of *office*, when, under the impression of that love which passeth knowledge, he cried out: "Behold! what manner of love the FATHER hath bestowed upon us, that we should be called the sons of God!" (1 John iii. 1.)

to shew the authority on which they rest. But as my present design is of another nature, and intended only to prevent your minds from being led away by an opinion injurious to Christianity, and advanced by Christians themselves, who acknowledge with us the writings of the New Testament to be genuine, it is not necessary, upon this occasion, to bring forward any evidence in their support. Taking it for granted, therefore, that the sacred volume is admitted to be authentic, I shall immediately proceed to bring before you that great body of evidence with which the Scriptures abound, to prove the deity of the Son of God, and that Jesus is, in the fullest sense of the expression, "one with the Father—over all, God blessed for ever. Amen."

The words of the text which I have thought to be most pertinent to the purpose of opening the subject on the divinity of Christ, are not a little demonstrative of the great point in question.

Our blessed Lord had been interrogated by the Pharisees and Sadducees, (and it should seem not with the most friendly design,) upon certain matters of opinion peculiar to each sect. After this conference, Jesus himself proposed to them the question in the text: "What think ye of Christ? whose son is he? They say unto him, The son of David. He saith unto them, How then doth David in spirit call him Lord; saying, The Lord said unto my Lord, Sit thou on my right hand, until I make thine enemies thy foot-stool? If David then call him Lord, how is he his son?" Let any man of plain common understanding read this passage as it stands in the New Testament, and then determine for himself; will it not instantly strike him, that our blessed Lord meant to infer, that somewhat above the nature of an human being was appointed to distinguish the character of the Messiah? That, notwithstanding Christ, according to the flesh, was to spring from the seed of David, yet, at the same time, by his superior nature, he was to be David's Lord. That our Saviour's argument was considered in this light by his hearers, and that it wrought a conviction of this kind upon their minds, seems highly probable; for the Evangelist adds, "They were not able to answer him a word, neither durst any man, from that day forth, ask him any more questions."

But passing by this argument in favour of our cause, I lay no stress upon it. It is the question only in the text which I wish to make use of as the basis of this discourse: "What think ye of Christ? whose son is he?" Is he, according to the opinion of our modern Socinians, simply no other than a man; or, agreeable to the doctrine of the Scriptures, is he the Son of God? This is the great and interesting question to be discussed in the prosecution of this subject. And my sincere prayers to God are, that void of all party persuasion, and unbiassed by the smallest prejudice, our researches may be directed by the influence of that blessed Spirit of truth, "which will guide us into all truth."

To a mind perfectly free from prepossession, and open to conviction, the numberless passages we meet with in Scripture, which fully and unequivocally declare Christ to be the Son of God, might, one would think, decidedly prove his Godhead. For such a distinguished and peculiar appellation cannot, with the smallest shadow of reason, be applied to him, unless his pretensions to the relationship it includes be also admitted.

Some, however, who have considered our blessed Lord in a higher degree of dignity than any prophet or messenger of God who preceded him; have yet conceived that nothing valid to the argument can be derived from this phrase of "Son of God," with which Christ is every where distinguished in the sacred writings. And, among other reasons, they have assigned that this title is sometimes given also in Scripture to angels, to magistrates,* and even good Christians.† It is wonderful that men of the most penetrating abilities should not immediately perceive the very dissimilar circumstances under which this appellation is used when applied to men, and when spoken of him who is not only said to be "the Son of God;" but declared to be the Son of God "with power;" and also "the express image of his person," (Rom. i. 4. Heb. i. 3.) They who are so ready to class our Lord's pretensions to this title with those of the general mass of eminent persons to whom it is sometimes given, would be at a loss, I believe, to explain, upon the same principles, in what sense we are to understand the term when it is connected with the most expressive phrases, such as "the only begotten Son of God who was in the bosom of the Father;" the "beloved Son of God," and "dear Son of God, the image of the invisible God, the first-born of every creature," (John i. 14—18. Matthew iii. 17. Mark ix. 7; Luke ix. 35. Colossians i. 13—15.) There must be something surely peculiar in those instances, and different from the common acceptation of the phrase when conferred by way of eminence on particular persons or characters. But, added to these striking particularities, there are other corroborating circumstances, which put the matter beyond all doubt, and which I shall much wonder if the most extravagant latitude of construction can possibly do away.

If I can prove to your satisfaction that this distinguished title, by which Christ is every where, in the New Testament, called the Son of God, was not applied to him merely by his followers, but was the

* In the book of Psalms, lxxxii. 6. "I have said, Ye are gods, and ye are all the children of the Most High."

† "As many as are led by the Spirit of God, they are the sons of God," Rom. viii. 14. And again, the apostle John says, "But as many as received him, to them gave he power to become the sons of God. Now are we the sons of God," 1 John iii. 2.

individual character by which his commission and authority were to be made known; that it was first declared by the angel in his address to Mary at the annunciation; afterwards assumed by our Lord himself at his entrance upon his public character; received the testimony of a voice from heaven, in confirmation of its truth, more than once, during our Lord's exercise of his ministry; and that even the spirits of darkness gave the same evidence to it: in short that this title uniformly characterized his person while he continued upon earth, and is the distinguishing name by which the apostles and inspired writers have revealed his doctrines to all ages of the church; and that these facts do not depend upon a single passage of a questionable sense or meaning, but that one invariable strain of testimony runs through the whole volume of Scripture. If, I say, I can shew this, I should hope it would be conclusive and satisfactory to every candid person. Permit me, therefore, to bring before you the several testimonies of this kind by which this leading proof of Christ's divinity is confirmed and assured.

The first instance is that of the angel in his salutation of Mary: "The Holy Ghost shall come upon thee, and the power of the Highest shall overshadow thee; THEREFORE that holy thing which shall be born of thee shall be called the Son of God," (Luke i. 35.) Now here is an express and positive reason assigned why Jesus is called the Son of God: from the Holy Ghost coming upon Mary, and the power of the Highest overshadowing her; by which our blessed Lord, deriving his existence in the flesh from a Divine Power, and without the intervention of an human father, he was truly and properly called the Son of God. A circumstance evidently peculiar to Christ, and by which the title becomes applicable only to him. Had the conception not been miraculous, but the natural consequence of Mary's marriage with her husband, there could have been no reason given for this appellation. There is something also very remarkable in the angel's expression: he does not say in consequence of this overshadowing power of the Highest "the child" shall be called the Son of God, but (το αγιον) "that holy thing;" thereby drawing a striking distinction between the Word made flesh, and the highest created being whatever.

The second proof I shall bring of Christ's exclusive claim to this title, personally considered, is the testimony of a voice from heaven, both at his baptism, and again at his transfiguration: "This is my beloved Son, in whom I am well pleased," (Matthew iii. 17. xviii. 5, &c. Luke ix. 35. Mark ix.) This, also, I conceive to be another very striking discrimination between the ordinary custom observable among men, whereby eminent persons may be distinguished by eminent titles; and the authority of a voice from heaven, giving so extraordinary a demonstration of the dignity of him to whom it was applied. If it can be any where shewn, and in any one instance, that any individual among the sons of men ever received such a testimony from above, then this of Jesus at his baptism and transfiguration will by so much be lessened upon a comparison in its importance: but if not, and it be clearly proved that CHRIST and CHRIST only was so distinguished, it plainly follows, that there must have been something peculiar in *his* person and character, from his receiving such supernatural attestations of his dignity and consequence. For we may venture to ask, in the words of the apostle, "Unto which of the angels said he at any time, Thou art my Son, this day have I begotten thee?" (Hebrews i. 5.)

But, thirdly, we have other testimony beside that of the angel, and a voice from above, for the spirits of darkness brought their unwilling evidence to the same great truth. Read only the latter part of the fourth chapter of the gospel by St. Luke, and then determine on what ground it is that Christ is called the Son of God. "And in the synagogue there was a man which had a spirit of an unclean devil, and he cried with a loud voice, saying, Let us alone, what have we to do with thee, thou Jesus of Nazareth; art thou come to destroy us? I know thee who thou art, the Holy One of God. And devils also came out of many, crying out, and saying, Thou art Christ, the Son of God. And he, rebuking them, suffered them not to speak, for they knew that he was Christ," (Luke vi. 41. Mark v.) What overpowering evidences are these collectively considered, that the appellation of this title given to Christ is peculiar and appropriate! How any man can possibly withhold his assent to the GODHEAD of Jesus, when even apostate spirits cannot refrain, is unaccountable and surprising.*

When we add to these strong testimonies the further evidence, that our blessed Lord assumed this title himself, and founded his mission expressly upon it, because he was the Son of God; this at once determines the whole, by clearly shewing that it is on his own declarations we are authorized to apply the sacred appellation to him; and

---

* It is an awful consideration, and may well merit the serious reflection of a retired hour, by way of humiliation to the pride of the human understanding; that the fall of man hath induced an effect of ignorance in the faculties, which "the angels that kept not their first estate" have not experienced, to their intellectual apprehension, in consequence of their apostacy. They, though fallen, know Christ, and readily confess his divinity and power. But man, with all his boasted knowledge, by nature, knows him not, neither can be brought, by all the efforts of mere reason only, to a clear apprehension of his person and character. While the "devils believe and tremble," we are solemnly assured by One who could not be mistaken, that "no man knoweth the Son but the Father; neither knoweth any man the Father save the Son, and he to whomsoever the Son will reveal him," Matt. ii. 27.

from hence we have reason also to infer, that the expression carries with it all the idea that we can entertain of a divine and eternal nature. It would be tedious to particularize every instance we meet with in the history of our blessed Lord of this kind, Let a few passages suffice.

Christ had healed a cripple on the Sabbath-day; for which the Jews sought to slay him; but Jesus answered them, "My Father worketh hitherto, and I work;" therefore the Jews sought the more to kill him, because "he not only had broken the Sabbath, but had said also, that God was his Father, making himself equal with God," (John v. 17, 18.) A most positive proof this, that our blessed Lord assumed this title, and that the Jews understood it in the light of a claim and of equality with the Father, for which they were so exceedingly exasperated against him.

Sometime after this, in a conference which Christ held with the Jews, in which he declared his unity with the Father, "I and my Father are one," they took up stones again to stone him; but Jesus demanded the cause for which they did it; they replied, "for blasphemy, because that thou, being a man, makest thyself God," (John x. 30, 33.) Can any thing be more in point than this?

Again, upon a similar occasion, when Christ had opened the eyes of one that was born blind, and much altercation and dispute arose between the Jews and the man in consequence of it, which terminated in putting him out of the synagogue, our blessed Lord met his patient, and proposed to him this very question, "Dost thou believe on the Son of God? He answered and said, Who is he, Lord, that I might believe on him? And Jesus said, Thou hast both seen him, and he it is that talketh with thee. And he said, Lord, I believe. And he worshipped him," (John ix. 35—38.) Here is an evidence the most express, plain, and positive that can be, and attended also with the divine adoration of Jesus. Would Christ have assumed this title, and accepted homage and worship by virtue of it, had not both been his just right? Would not this meek and humble Saviour rather have corrected the errors of the man, and availed himself of so good an opportunity of renouncing such a title, and enjoining the worship of God only, had not his divinity been unquestionable, and his relationship to the Father fully clear and indisputable? Judge then on what dangerous ground those men tread, who step forward with so much confidence to rob the Son of God of his due, and endeavour to degrade the eternal Son of the Father to the condition of a poor being like ourselves! What a different opinion the apostle Peter had of his Master's real character, and what sentiments he entertained of our Lord's claim to this title, may easily be gathered from the expressions he made use of in his way to Cæsarea Philippi. When Christ, in order to try their faith in him, proposed to his disciples this question, "Whom do men say that I, the Son of man am? They said, Some say that thou art John the Baptist; some Elias; and others, Jeremias, or one of the Prophets." And when Christ desired to know what they thought of him, Peter, with his usual promptness, immediately cried out, "Thou art Christ the Son of the living God." Can any man suppose that this was said in compliment only? That Peter would say to a man like himself, Thou art Christ the Son of the living God? Is it possible any one can adopt such an opinion? and especially when it procured for him that glorious commendation, "Blessed art thou, Simon Barjona, for flesh and blood hath not revealed it unto thee, but my Father which is in heaven," (Matt. xvi. 13.) So far indeed was this from being a common compliment, used in courtesy to distinguish men, that Christ declared it to be a truth of that superlative nature, that human discernment was unequal to the discovery of it; and it could only be revealed by God the Father. The same divine truth, it may justly be said, operates in the present hour. "The natural man receiveth not the things of the Spirit of God, for they are foolishness to him, neither can he know them, because they are spiritually discerned," (1 Cor. ii. 14.)

I shall mention only one passage more, in confirmation of our Lord's assumption of this title; and that is the instance at his trial, when the high-priest demanded of Jesus, by a solemn adjuration, to tell him, "whether he were the Christ the Son of God," (Luke xxii. 70,) or as the equivalent phrase of another Evangelist expresses it, "Art thou the Christ, the Son of the Blessed?" (Mark xiv. 61.) And on our Lord's declaring that he was, the high-priest rent his clothes, saying, he had spoken blasphemy. Would he have pronounced this blasphemy, if it had been considered as nothing more than a usual complimentary title given to remarkable characters *ex officio*? Much less would he have declared Jesus deserving of death in consequence of it? Is it not self-evident, that the Jews considered the expression in the full sense and acceptation of the word; and which, of consequence, became blasphemy, if improperly assumed? And is it not equally clear that Christ laid down his life in support of his just pretensions to this title?

Such repeated proofs of the point in question, leave no room to doubt in what sense we are to consider Christ's assumption of his character, and what ideas we are to annex to this distinguished appellation. It must be plain to every candid and unprejudiced mind, that the term made use of, when applied to the person of Jesus, differs most essentially when used in compliment to any other among the sons of men. And if we have authority to draw any inference from any one fact in the world, we may with the fullest safety conclude, from those instances, that our blessed Lord is, in the highest and most complete sense of the word, "the Son of God." Here the reasoning of the apostle is strictly applicable; "If we receive the witness of men, the witness of God is greater, and this is the witness of God which he hath testified of his Son," (John i. 5—9.)

It were unnecessary for me to go further, and enumerate the several passages we meet with in Scripture, in which Christ is particularly distinguished by this title among his apostles and followers. After the review already taken, and especially our Lord's own testimony on this point, it would, I think, be superfluous.* Even

* Though it were needless to multiply quotations, in support of the doctrine before us, yet, as some of the expressions with which Christ is particularized, under the character of "Son of God," are singularly striking, it may not be amiss to mention a few of them in a note. The apostle Paul, when speaking of Christ, says, that "he was declared to be the Son of God with power," Rom. i. 4. Had Christ's resurrection been solely the effect of the Father, or the Holy Ghost's operation, the resurrection of Christ in this sense would not have declared him to be the Son of God with power, no more than the resurrection of others. But when it is said, as in this Scripture, that he was declared to be the Son of God with power, "by his resurrection from the dead;" this act of His proved his eternal power and Godhead. And the apostle plainly testified by this expression, what the apostle's sentiments were, that this appellation was not with Christ a barren title, but accompanied with that plenitude of authority which the relationship might be supposed to include; differing most essentially in every point when applied to any mere human character, and when spoken of Him who came in all the power of the Highest.

The testimony of Nathaniel is to the same amount also; for it was given upon our Lord's displaying proofs of his divine omniscience. "Rabbi, (says he) thou art the Son of God," John i. 49.

The apostle Peter, upon a remarkable occasion, hath given us his repeated ideas of this title; "Lord, to whom shall we go? (says he) thou hast the words of eternal life, and we believe and are sure that thou art the Christ, the Son of the living God," John vi. 69.

Martha, in making profession of her faith, used these memorable words, "I believe, (says she) that thou art the Christ, the Son of God, which should come into the world," John xi. 27.

what hath been now advanced on this subject, I would wish to be considered only as collateral to the main body of evidence which I purpose to bring forward in discussing the important question of our Lord's divinity.

I cannot but think the several circumstances I have laid before you, respecting the phrase itself when applied to our Saviour, are very striking and particular; but they are not so essential to our cause as to oblige us to lay the greatest stress upon them. The argument arising from hence, and much more, I think, we might

---

And the apostle John, in the conclusion of his gospel, tells us, that the works and miracles of Christ which he hath recorded, were written on purpose "that ye might believe that Jesus is the Christ, the Son of God, and that believing, ye might have life through his name," John xx. 31. All which demonstrate most fully, that when Jesus is called the "Son of God," it is in a very different sense from the meaning when applied to any other character. Philip the Deacon, it is evident, considered it to be so when his Æthiopian convert made profession of his belief as a qualification for baptism: "I believe (says he) that Jesus is the Son of God," Acts viii. 37. If this implied no more than a mere complimentary form, he might as well have professed his belief in any other remarkable character of Scripture.—And that the name of "Son of God," given to Christ upon all these occasions, is not merely titular, is abundantly strengthened in the proof by the divine attributes annexed to his character. When we behold these essential properties of divinity; omnipotency, omnisciency, and the like, ascribed to Jesus (as hereafter will be shewn,) it is not all the art of man that can apply these to any thing official.

From these and other passages of the like nature, which might, if needful, have been brought into the argument, nothing, I think, can be more plain, than that the apostles, and first followers of Christianity, considered our Lord, in the fullest sense, the real and proper Son of God. And I must confess it is with astonishment, that I behold men, who acknowledge the divine authority of Christ's mission, and yet disallow, at the same time, his claim to a divine character, which he evidently assumed. For surely it was incompatible with the pure and humble spirit of Jesus, to have taken, or even permitted, such a title to have been applied to him, if all the while he was conscious he had no right or claim to it. Such notions would never have been cherished in his holy breast. But what an awful passage is that of the apostle John, to those who reject, *in toto*, all the evidences with which this truth is supported! "He that believeth not God, hath made him a liar, because he believeth not the record that God gave of his Son," John i. 5—10.

with safety give up, and yet retain enough to prove the doctrine I am anxious to confirm in your minds.

The Godhead of Jesus is so conspicuous a feature in the gospel, and is supported by evidences which press upon us so closely on every side, that, I am sure, there is not any one point of Christ's religion more capable of being clearly proved and ascertained, than his claim to a divine nature.

I should proceed immediately to the testimonies contained in Scripture of this great doctrine, but their importance demands a more full and particular discussion than your present attention will permit. I reserve them, therefore, for the subject of our next meeting. In the mean time, consider what hath been said, and may the Lord give you a right understanding in all things.

SERMON II.

JOHN XVII. 5.

The glory which I had with thee before the world was.

THE prominent features which discriminated the life of Jesus, when upon earth, from all other characters which have at any time appeared upon the stage of this world, will be placed in the most advantageous point of view, if we previously examine the evidences we have of his pre-existent state and dignity. These, no doubt, are the great *criteria* of his divinity, and can alone enable us to comprehend many of the august events which followed in his life. My chief object in the present sermon, therefore, will be to collect such accounts as we have of this doctrine in Scripture, and bring them before you, together with the evidences of our Lord's character, as described by the sacred writers; which will tend, I hope, greatly to ascertain, and prove beyond all doubt, his right to a divine nature.

It would swell the subject to an unusual length, and much exceed the limits allotted to addresses of this kind, were I to instance every passage in the writings of the Evangelists and Apostles, which refers to this important point. I shall content myself, therefore, with selecting such only as are more immediately pertinent to my purpose, and of the plainest and most obvious meaning.

Happy indeed is it for mankind, that many of them are self-evident, and require no explanation. The word of God, which is intended for common use, is adapted to common apprehension. And though it is written with all the marks of the most consummate wisdom, yet it wonderfully condescends, at the same time, to the humblest capacities, particularly in the great and essential points of knowledge, in which there is nothing but what the most uninformed mind through grace is capable of receiving. Divine goodness in this, as well as many other instances, plainly shewing, that however these things may be hid from the wise and prudent, yet hath he revealed them unto babes.* "God hath chosen

---

* Matthew xi. 25. I have often thought, what an awakening consideration ariseth out of the doctrine contained in these words of Jesus: that sacred truths are "hidden from the wise and prudent," while they are "revealed unto babes." And when from the written word, we look into the world, for the evidences of the fact, and find such a wonderful correspondence between them; when we see men of the first abilities in *human* learning, the merest novices in *divine* things; while among the illiterate and uneducated, in the humbler walks of life, we as frequently discover a proficiency, and even depth of knowledge, in that science, which maketh "wise unto salvation;" the mind is awfully impressed in the review, and cannot help being led, almost instinctively as it were, to confess that there must be some more than ordinary cause operating to such events. Whatever the predisposing means are, the fact itself is undeniable; the peculiar and distinguishing truths of the gospel, are hidden from the wise and prudent, though revealed unto babes. As the matter is not altogether irrelevant to the interesting subject we are upon, it will not be considered, I should hope, an unpardonable digression, if I offer an observation in this way upon it. I should not have thought it proper to have interrupted the progress of the subject itself, by introducing it in the body of the Sermon; but in a note it is not, I conceive, so liable to objection.

By the fall of man, there is in every son and daughter of Adam, not only a total disinclination to the study of divine things; but a total inability, until restored by sovereign grace to a new and spiritual life in Christ, to the apprehension of them. "The natural man receiveth not the things of the SPIRIT of GOD, for they are foolishness unto him; neither can he know them, because they are spiritually discerned," 1 Cor. ii. 14. Observe, it is said, he *cannot* know them; because, being by nature dead in trespasses and sins, until regenerated, and spiritual life given unto him in CHRIST, he hath no spiritual faculties by which he might receive spiritual things. He is as incapable of spiritual food, as a dead man of animal sustenance. Hence, the solemn words of CHRIST, "Ye must be born again," John iii. 7. Until this Almighty act is wrought, the sinner, though he hears with the bodily ear, the great truths of GOD, neither can discern them, nor receive them. Hence, no less than *seven*

the foolish things of the world (saith an apostle) to confound the wise, and the weak things of the world to confound the mighty," (1 Cor. i. 27.)

Nothing can more strikingly prove this, than the several passages of Scripture which have a reference to our present argument. For example, we see the most positive and express declaration of Christ's pre-existence and dignity in the words of the text. For when our blessed Lord says, "he had glory with the Father before the world was," what possible conclusion can any man make of this, but that Christ had existence in glory with the Father before the world? No sophistry or evasion can do away the very evident sense of the phrase. It is likely many different opinions may arise in the minds of different persons concerning the nature and degree of the glory here spoken of; and men fond of disputation and argument may spend much time in conjectures upon it: but if the words of Christ himself can be supposed to have any sense or meaning, his pre-existence and connexion with the Father must be admitted. "He had glory with the Father before the world was."* Nor could so plain a passage of Scrip-

---

times in scripture, the HOLY GHOST hath recorded those awful words: "Go, and tell this people, Hear ye indeed, but understand not; and see ye indeed, but perceive not." Isaiah vi. 9; Matt. xiii. 14; Mark iv. 12; Luke viii. 10; John xii. 40; Acts xxviii. 26; Romans xi. 9.

* I detain the reader for a moment to ponder these sublime words. They were spoken by the LORD JESUS, and spoken to the FATHER. And there are these two most blessed but most mysterious things folded up in them, which baffle all our intellectual faculties to explain; namely, "He had glory with the FATHER before the world." And 2ndly, He saith, "And now, O FATHER, glorify thou me with thine own self with the glory which I had with thee before the world was." John xvii. 5.) Now here are several striking particulars. First, His own *essential* glory which he had in common with the FATHER, and the HOLY GHOST. 2dly, He desires that he might be glorified by the FATHER "with his own self:" and this is evidently as GOD and Man Mediator; for the *essential* glory of GODHEAD was, and is, his own, and never to be asked for, nor given. And, 3dly, here is implied a some-

ture ever have been thought ambiguous, were it not that, passing by the first, and most obvious meaning, men suffer themselves to be led away in quest of something more mysterious than the plain sense naturally suggests.

So again, when our blessed Lord, upon various occasions, expressed himself on this subject, and without a figure, in words like these; "I came down from heaven," (John vi. 38.) I proceeded forth, and came from God," (John viii. 42.) "Before Abraham was, I am,"* (John viii. 58.) "No man hath ascended up to heaven but he that came down from heaven, even the Son of man who is in heaven," (John iii. 13.) And in a conference with the Jews, he contrasted his nature and character with theirs, in language liable to no misconception; "Ye are from beneath, I am from above. Ye are of this world, I am not of this world," (John viii. 23.) "What, and if ye shall see the Son of Man ascend up where he was before?" (John viii. 62.) What construction can any one possibly put upon these very plain phrases that shall deprive them of their evident sense and meaning, "that Christ came down from heaven," and that "he proceeded, and came forth from God."

---

what of glory as Mediator, even glorified by the FATHER "with his own self;" which as it was before the world, so will it be, when there is no world; and to which none of the members of his mystical body can attain. And this is again expressed by the LORD, John vi. 46; "Not that any man hath seen the FATHER, save he which is of GOD, he hath seen the FATHER!" Hence it follows, that that holy portion of our nature, by being taken into union with one of the Persons in the GODHEAD, possesseth all divine faculties, so as to see JEHOVAH in his Trinity of Persons, who is himself invisible to all his creatures. What a view doth this one scripture give of the infinite greatness of our GOD and Saviour?

* It is worthy to be remarked, that the same phrase, *I am*, is made use of by Christ in the 24th verse of this chapter, and an awful denunciation added to it; "If ye believe not that I am, ye shall die in your sins." Our translators, by the addition of the pronoun *he*, have very much enervated, if not totally altered, the sense of the expression. The original is, εαν γαρ με πιστευσετε οτι εγο ειμι, &c.

It must be, I conceive, departing exceedingly wide from the point intended, to reduce them into mere figure and metaphor. That the apostles of Christ accepted them in their literal sense is evident; for upon an occasion of this kind, when our blessed Lord was discoursing to them upon the subject, and expressed himself in much the same language, "I came forth from the Father, and am come into the world: again, I leave the world, and go to the Father," (John xvi. 28,) his disciples acknowledged that Christ spake plainly, and spake not to them in proverbs; and they expressed their faith in this doctrine in terms which, one would have thought, might have been safely followed by all sincere professors of Christianity to the end of the world: "Now (say they) are we sure that thou knowest all things, and needest not that any man should ask thee: by this we believe that thou camest forth from God," (John xvi. 30.)

Once more. When the apostle John says, in one of his epistles, "We know the Son of God is come:" and again, in his gospel, "The Word was made flesh, and dwelt among us; and we beheld his glory, the glory as of the only begotten of the Father:" in both these passages the meaning is liable to no misapprehension, upon the supposition of Christ's eternal nature; but the whole is abundantly clear, intelligible, and not to be mistaken. But put this out of the question, how ridiculous and absurd would it be to say, "the Son of God is come," if Christ was not really and truly the Son of God, and did not possess an exclusive privilege to this title? or, why should the apostle particularize so plain and obvious a proposition, that "the Word was made flesh, and dwelt among us," if our Lord was simply no other than a human being, and never existed before his birth from the Virgin Mary? How should a human being be otherwise made than in *flesh?* And whom should he dwell with but with men? Above all, what possible claim could this man of flesh have to the dignity mentioned;

the glory which was beheld in him, as of "the only begotten of the Father?" Either I am greatly deceived, or there are many absurdities and even contradictions, in attempting to reconcile those phrases with the Socinian creed! And yet it should seem, nothing can be more plain and evident than those passages of Scripture are, when read without prejudice, and accepted in their first and most obvious meaning.

And here I cannot help digressing one moment, just to observe, how necessary it must be for all Christians who are sincerely desirous of coming to the knowledge of the truth, carefully to consult the sacred volume, in its pure and uncorrupt state, and in its own beautiful simplicity and plainness, unaltered by commentators of any description. It was the commendation given to the Thessalonians by the apostle Paul, that when "they received the word of God, they received it not as the word of men, but as it is in truth, the word of God, which effectually worketh in them that believe," (1 Thess. ii. 13.)

But I proceed to the further selection of those passages of Scripture which more particularly point out the pre-existence and dignity of our blessed Lord.

Among the many evidences of this kind, the exordium of St. John's gospel claims our first attention; for it is so much to our purpose, and confirms so decidedly this great article of our faith, that, if the authority of an inspired writer can be at all considered as conclusive or satisfactory, we need no further quotation in proof of it. Either it establishes the fact itself by indisputable testimony, or it must be considered as introducing the sacred contents which follow in his gospel, by a falsehood and contradiction in the very preface. "In the beginning was the Word, and the Word was with God, and the Word was God; the same was in the beginning with God." This memorable passage, which so fully and circumstantially asserts the divinity of Jesus (by ascribing to him such attributes as are only compatible with

Godhead), hath been examined with the most nice and scrupulous criticism, from the days of the apostles to the present hour, in order to invalidate the meaning, and to prove, if possible, that by the term *Word*, the sacred writer intended nothing personal. But all attempts of this kind must be insufficient. For when the apostle so plainly declares, that the Word was not only in the beginning *with* God, but actually *was* God, surely nothing can be more decisive: for this would be utterly impossible without admitting a personality. And, as if to remove all objections, and that no doubt might remain concerning the true sense of the word, it is remarkable, that the same apostle (who must be supposed the best commentator on himself), uses the same expression in one of his epistles, and there annexes such positive qualities to the term as fully decide the point in question. "That (says he) which was from the beginning, which we have heard, which we have seen with our eyes, which we have looked upon, and our hands have handled of the word of life." Terms these, highly expressive of person, and impossible to be accepted in any other sense. And observe how striking to the purpose what follows: "For the life (says he) was manifested, and we have seen it, and bear witness, and shew unto you that eternal life which was with the Father, and was manifested unto us." (1 John i. 1, 2.) "That eternal life;" what a sublime expression! which not only confirms the certainty of its being personal, but also proves, according to the apostle's ideas, the eternal nature of Him to whom it belongs. Both which are well known to refer to our Lord Jesus Christ. So conclusive and satisfactory are the writings of this beloved apostle in the very exordium both of his gospel and epistle, on this important doctrine. And were not facts against it, I should think it impossible that any one could open the Testament to these chapters, and read them with an unprejudiced mind, who could close the book without the fullest conviction of the divinity of Jesus.

Again: the apostle Paul exhorting the Corinthians to charity, makes use of the following remarkable passage: "Ye know the grace of our Lord Jesus Christ, that though he was rich, yet for your sakes he became poor, that ye through his poverty might be rich," (2 Cor. viii. 9.) In this verse the apostle plainly refers to a point which he assumes as a thing unquestionable, and which the Corinthians were not only informed of, but believed; namely, the dignity of Christ, previous to his appearance in the flesh. For otherwise the expression is unwarrantable and false. Christ we know was born and bred in the humblest poverty, and from the first hour of his entrance into the world, to his departure out of it, respecting worldly circumstances, was most poor, and wretched indeed: how then could the apostle call him rich? It is, therefore, clear that he alludes to that glory which Christ himself tells us he had with the Father before the world was, and which he put off when he came upon earth. And it is still more worthy your observation, that the apostle refers this to the consideration of the Corinthians, not as a new matter which they had never heard of before, or was at all questioned, or disputed among them, but as a fact with which they were all well acquainted, and which no man denied: "Ye *know* (says he) the grace of our Lord Jesus Christ, that though he was rich," &c.

Once more; the same apostle, in his Epistle to the Philippians, hath a passage equally demonstrative of this doctrine. "Let this mind be in you, which was also in Christ Jesus: who, being in the form of God, thought it not robbery to be equal with God: but made himself of no reputation, and took upon him the form of a servant, and was made in the likeness of men: and being found in fashion as a man, he humbled himself and became obedient unto death, even the death of the cross," (Phil. ii. 5, *et seq.*) I am perfectly aware what a variety of constructions has been put upon this memorable passage of Scripture, and how different a sense has been made of it, so as to make it correspond to the particular tenets of different denominations of Christians. Melancholy proof of human infirmity! But let commentators be ever so widely divided in opinion as to certain expressions contained in it; whether, when the apostle says, "Christ was in the form of God," he meant a full, and absolute equality, as some have insisted on, or whether he meant that Christ was in the form only, and his dignity of a subordinate and secondary nature, as others have supposed; give the most unbounded scope to the expression you please, yet all the freedom of translation in the world cannot do away the evident sense of one fact there asserted, namely, that Christ *was* in the form of God, before he made himself of no reputation, and took upon him the form of a servant; of consequence it follows, that our blessed Lord had an antecedent state to his humiliation, and appearance in the flesh: so that his being and existence will remain unquestionable, whatever meaning shall be assigned to the phrase of "being in the form of God." Admit, therefore (what on these premises cannot, I think, be denied), that the words of the apostle fairly express this doctrine, and this is all I am contending for at present. Much more, I am convinced, might be made of this passage of Scripture, for it certainly contains great information of our Lord's dignity and character. But these points will more properly meet us under another part of the subject.

From the several quotations of Scripture which have now been brought before you, the first point I had in view to prove, namely, our Lord's pre-existence, is, I hope, fully established. You are in possession of an authority which hath ever been held sacred and unquestionable. And it now remains with you, under the light of grace, to determine for yourselves the sufficiency of the evidence. The passages I have selected from others of a similar meaning (and which, if needful, might have been subjoined), are of the plainest nature, and such as I think cannot easily be misunderstood. Let me beg of you, therefore, to read them only with a proper attention and with a cool unprejudiced mind, and accept them in the sense which is most obvious, and such as every candid person would naturally take them in. And, if the Lord be your teacher, I would venture to rest the cause I am pleading upon the event of their testimony, so clear and explicit are they, in support of this important article of our faith.

But this doctrine will receive a further confirmation, by an evidence still more striking and palpable, when we proceed to consider our blessed Lord under those great and distinguishing attributes in which the sacred writers have presented him, as the *Creator* and *Preserver* of the universe.

All the works of the creation are expressly ascribed to Christ, in many parts of Scripture; and as these are the greatest acts of omnipotency we know of, or can conceive, so do they afford the most positive assurance of his GODHEAD.

The same gospel of St. John, which expresses the pre-existence of the Eternal Word with the Father, speaks of him, at the same time, as the Creator of the universe. For, after saying that the Word was in the beginning with God, and was God, he immediately adds, "All things were made by him." And, as if this were not sufficiently expressive, he repeats the same truth in a more full and comprehensive manner, by declaring, that "without him was not any thing made that was made." Thus raising our ideas of the omnipotency of Christ to the most exalted height, in clothing him with those great and distinguishing attributes of the Deity. The same truth is assorted again in a subsequent verse, when he tells us, " that he was in the world, and the world was made by him, and the world knew him not," (John i. 2; iii. 10.) No form of words can more fully testify the power of Christ than the works which are here so plainly ascribed to him; and as these operations of our Lord are equal to the highest conceptions we can possibly frame of a divine being, the consequence is evident, that Christ possessed a divine nature. "His eternal power and Godhead (as the apostle Paul observes), are clearly seen, being understood by the things that are made," (Romans i. 20.)

But it is not on the testimony of one apostle only that we ground our belief that Christ is the Creator of the universe; there are others of the sacred writers which confirm the same doctrine.

The author of the epistle to the Hebrews, in his first chapter, both ascribes the works of creation and preservation to our Lord, and speaks of him under such great and distinguishing characters, as are altogether irreconcilable with common sense, upon any other idea than that Christ possessed all the attributes of the Godhead. " God (says he), who at sundry times, and in divers manners, spake in time past unto the fathers, by the prophets, hath in these last days spoken unto us by his Son, whom he hath appointed heir of all things, by whom also he made the worlds. Who being the brightness of his glory, and the express image of his person, and upholding all things by the word of his power." Words surely as full, and expressive of the divinity of Jesus, as language is capable of furnishing, and which it would be little less than blasphemy to apply to any created being whatever. Indeed this whole chapter is so replete with terms denoting the omnipotency and eternity of Christ, and ascribing to him every divine honour, that the sacred writer seems to labour for expression to describe the dignity and greatness of his person. He calls our Lord the Son of God, the " brightness of his glory," and "the express image of his person;" of a nature "superior to angels," and most essentially different from all the servants of God, whether prophets or ministering spirits, whether angels or men, which have been sent forth to minister unto them who are the heirs of salvation; the "Creator and Upholder of all things; an Eternal Being, whose throne is for ever and ever;" and whom at his first entrance into the world the angels of God were commanded to worship. When I behold the blessed Redeemer of the universe thus described, under the power of inspiration, as possessing all the peculiar attributes of the GODHEAD, I am astonished how any man who professes to receive the holy Scriptures as the guide of his faith, can behold this divine person so clearly, and circumstantially pointed out, under such great and eternal characters, and yet consider him still as a created being. What language or expressions could the sacred writer have made use of, to convey to us, in stronger terms than he has done, the certainty of our Lord's divinity? Every verse of this chapter seems more or less expressive of it; and so much to the purpose is the whole taken together, that if this convinces not, all further application to Scripture on this point, I fear, will be superfluous and vain.

But though these passages might be sufficient to answer my present argument, and I trust your faith needs no further reference, in order to establish your hearts firm in the persuasion that our Lord is the Creator of the universe; yet, as it cannot but be gratifying to every sincere believer in this important doctrine, to find the truth of it attested in many other parts of the New Testament, I shall add one or two more of the same kind with those we have already reviewed, for its confirmation.

In the third chapter of the Epistle to the Hebrews, the sacred writer draws a comparison between Moses the great lawgiver of the Old Covenant, and Jesus the

Mediator of the New, in order to point out the vast inferiority of the former, when brought in competition with the latter, by reason of the very different nature of their persons, and the different characters they sustained. "For this man," says he, "was counted worthy of more glory than Moses, inasmuch as he who hath builded a house hath more honour than the house, for every house is built by some man, but he that built all things is God," (Heb. iii. 3.) Now here is another decisive proof, and not easily to be mistaken, that the sacred writer considered Christ as the Creator of the world, and possessed a divinity equal to such an operation; adding, as an unavoidable inference from what he hath said, that "he who built all things must be God." And to confirm this still more, he proceeds, in the following verse, to point out in what that distinction, which so highly discriminated our Lord from Moses, did consist. "Moses," says he, "verily was faithful in all his house as a servant, but Christ as a son over his own house, whose house are we." This, it is true, is a figurative mode of expression, but so very plain as to require but little illustration. The apostle couches it under the image of an household, where God is considered as the Father of the family, and Christ the Son and heir. Moses, and all other messengers, whether angels, prophets, or apostles, are servants and attendants only. The superiority of our blessed Lord's character, and the divinity of his person, could hardly have been represented under any figure more apt or expressive than this; which so fully points out his relationship with the Father, and the essential line of distinction which must for ever take place between the son and heir of a family, and the highest order of servants whatever. Consider the character of Moses as it is mentioned in Scripture, and then behold him in the class of servants to our Lord, and you will require nothing more to shew you the very differnt characters they sustained, and, of consequence, the very different point of view in which they ought to be regarded. "There arose not a prophet since in Israel like unto Moses, whom the Lord knew face to face, in all the signs and the wonders which the Lord sent him to do in the land of Egypt, to Pharaoh, and to all his servants, and to all his land; and in all that mighty hand, and in all the great terror which Moses shewed in the sight of all Israel." Deut. xxxiv. 10—12.

So again, we read upon another occasion, the decided superiority of Moses over all prophets and messengers whom Jehovah ever sent, when Miriam and Aaron rebelled against the government of Moses, and assumed an equal authority with him. "Hath the Lord spoken only to him," say they, "hath he not spoken also by us?" The determination of God is full to the point. "If there be a prophet among you, I the Lord will make myself known unto him in a vision, and will speak unto him in a dream. My servant Moses is not so, who is faithful in all mine house. With him will I speak mouth to mouth, even apparently, and not in dark speeches; and the similitude of the Lord shall he behold: wherefore then were ye not afraid to speak against my servant Moses?" (Numb. xii. 6. *et seq.*) Such is the exalted description given in Scripture of this highly favoured servant of the Lord. But the apostle tells us, that this Moses, this mighty and greatest of all prophets which arose in Israel, when brought in comparison with Jesus was nothing. He was but a servant to Christ; and though faithful in all his house, "for a testimony of those things which were to be spoken after;" yet, in every point of view, he was subordinate to him who was a Son in his own house, "the brightness of his Father's glory, and the express image of his person." Can any thing with more pointed emphasis define the dignity of our blessed Lord's character?

You will not, I hope, think it trespassing too much

upon your time and patience, if I add to these testimonies one passage more from Scripture, in confirmation of the important doctrine we are considering; for it is peculiarly apposite to our purpose, and seems expressive of every particular by which the divinity of Jesus as an omnipotent Being can be illustrated and proved. The passage I allude to is in St. Paul's Epistle to the Colossians. In which, speaking of Jesus Christ, he thus expresses himself; "who is the image of the invisible God, the first-born of every creature.* By him were all things created that are in heaven, and that are in earth, visible and invisible, whether they be thrones, or dominions, or principalities, or powers. All things were created by him, and for him: and he is before all things, and by him all things consist."

This passage is most happily calculated to clear up every possible doubt (if any could yet remain) concerning the real dignity of our blessed Lord; and it is altogether so much to the purpose, that no form of words could have been brought within the same compass, equally strong and expressive to the point in question. It should seem, indeed, as though the apostle, by the spirit of prophecy, had foreseen the doubts and objections of certain Christians, and particularly directed his attention, in this place, to silence every scruple concerning our Lord's true character, by declaring his possession of such attributes as could only be consistent with true and proper divinity. For to shew Christ's pre-existence, he first styles him the "image of the invisible God, born or begotten before every creature."

* "First-born of every creature." I have preserved the phrase as it stands in our present translation, because I presume not to correct it; but it is well known, the original, which is πρωτοτοκος πασης κτισεως literally means the first-begotten before all creation; and the general sense of the verse clearly makes it so. For he who made all things in heaven and earth, must himself have had existence underived from creation.

To prove his possession of unlimited power, he next declares, that "all things were created by him:" and that no one, either through weakness or perversion, might misconstrue his sense and meaning, he goes on to prove, that Christ possessed this sovereign power inherently, and underived from another; for all things (he says) were not only created *by* him, but *for* him: thereby silencing all the arguments of those who allow Christ to have been the Creator of the world, yet regard him not as the efficient cause, but merely as the agent of his Father; whereas the apostle positively says, "All things were created by him, and for him." And still more, to put the matter beyond all doubt, he repeats the same truth again, in saying, that "by him do all things consist." And lastly, to remove all possible ideas of a local power circumscribed by space, or limited in operation to this world only, he tells us, that "by him were all things created that are in heaven, and that are in earth;" not simply material substances, such as our eyes behold, and no other, but immaterial, "visible and invisible:" and these not only of the lowest order, but even the highest and the best, "whether they be thrones, or dominions, or principalities, or powers: all without exception were created by him, and for him, and by him do all things consist." Thus, as with an indelible seal, the apostle, in this chapter, hath stamped the certainty of the divine nature of the blessed Redeemer of the world, ascribing such attributes and perfections to him, as are utterly irreconcilable with any possible idea of a created being, and can with justice be applied to none but the one true God.

I have now finished all the quotations from Scripture which I conceive to be necessary in proof of the great object I had in view in this discourse. And if the evidence of the inspired writers can be at all depended upon, no possible question will remain of the truth of what they have so positively asserted, that our Lord existed in a state of glory antecedent to his incarnation, and is the Creator and Preserver of the universe. And surely these perfections include such essential attributes of the Godhead, as fully prove our Lord's claim to this distinguished character. For (as an apostle justly reasons), "He who built all things is God."

When we behold the blessed Redeemer of the world revealed to us under such august and eternal distinctions, possesing an existence "in glory with his Father before all worlds," the Maker and Upholder of all things; is it possible to see our Lord thus represented, without being struck with horror at a presumption so dreadful as that of dethroning the Son of God, and reducing him to the level of a poor creature like ourselves? Would this meek and humble Saviour have arrogated to himself divine honours, unless his pretensions had been well founded? Or can any conceive that he would have declared he possessed glory with his Father, with other expressions of a similar nature, intimating his pre-existent state, when that existence began only at his incarnation? Much less would the apostles of such a Master have dared to apply to him the distinguishing characteristics of the supreme God, but upon the most perfect conviction of their justice and propiety.

Pause one moment, I beseech you, and seriously consider the importance of these questions. No act of omnipotence which our present faculties are capable of conceiving, surpasses the works of creation. And hence we find, in the Old Testament, when God is pleased to reveal himself to the Israelites, in order to impress their minds with a proper awe, and reverence of the astonishing greatness of his character; he refers them to the works of creation as proofs of his omnipotency, and calls upon them to draw a just and proper distinction between *his* eternal nature, and the perishable idols of the heathens around them. "Thus saith the Lord, who hath created the heavens, and stretched them out;

I am the Lord that maketh all things, that stretcheth forth the heavens alone, that spreadeth abroad the earth by myself. Before me there was no God formed, neither shall there be any after me. I, even I, am the Lord, and beside me there is no Saviour. Hast thou not known, hast thou not heard, that the everlasting God, the Lord, the Creator of the ends of the earth, fainteth not, neither is weary? To whom then will ye liken me, or shall I be equal, saith the Holy One? Behold the gods of the heathen are of nothing, and their works of nought: Produce your cause, saith the Lord, bring forth your strong reasons, saith the King of Jacob; Let them bring forth and shew us what shall happen, that we may know that ye are gods; yea, do good, or do evil, that we may be dismayed, and behold it together," (Isaiah xl. xli. &c.) In these, and the like awful characters, hath the Lord displayed the sovereignty of his power, as instanced in the works of the creation; and there is no one of the divine attributes so frequently referred to in the holy Scripture, in order to strike the mind of man with a proper conviction of the greatness of God, as this of his omnipotency. Probably because it is best suited to our present conceptions, which are most likely to be affected by great and magnificent objects.

But, perhaps, a difficulty may seem to arise, how to reconcile with each other those equivalent phrases, which ascribe the creation of the universe both to the Father and to the Son. If God the Father be thus clearly revealed in Scripture as the maker of all things, and if the same authority teach us to understand the same of the Son; how is this to be consistently explained? This difficulty is at once removed by a reference to the same unerring standard of truth, from whence we learn, that there is such an intimate union subsisting between the Father and the Son, that the acts of the one are equally the acts of the other: according to our

Lord's own account of this mystery, "Whatsoever works the Father doeth, these also doeth the Son," (John v. 19.) In short, the fact itself once admitted, that Christ is the Creator of all things, the doctrine of the divine unity will naturally be included. If you wish to go further, and question how, and in what manner this unity consists? here I remain silent; reason is incompetent to answer; and the word of God, which is our only guide in the mysterious points of religion, hath not condescended to inform us. Perhaps it was impossible to explain it in terms suitable to the apprehensions of mankind. It was thought sufficient, therefore, to give proofs of the fact itself, without accounting for the method by which this connection is preserved. Our Lord own declarations enable us to ascertain the certainty of the doctrine, but they leave the mind wholly at a loss to form any just idea of the manner of its operation. "I and my Father are one," (John x. 30.) "My Father worketh hitherto, and I work," (John v. 17.) "All things that the Father hath are mine," (John xvi. 15.) "I can do nothing of myself, but my Father which dwelleth in me, he doeth the works. "What things soever he doeth, these also doeth the Son likewise," (John v. 19.) These expressions very evidently determine the truth of the thing itself; but how, and in what way, this hypostatic union is preserved, I have not the smallest conception: no more than I can explain those equally mysterious passages of the apostle when he says, that "God was in Christ reconciling the world to himself," (2 Cor. v. 19.) "And in him (that is in Christ) dwelleth all the fulness of the Godhead bodily," (Col. ii. 9.) But when I trace, through every part of the sacred volume, the evident footsteps of a Being equal to all the ideas I can possibly frame of GODHEAD, in the person of Jesus Christ; and such actions as leave at an infinite distance every character among the sons of men; I am deeply smitten with the conviction of his divine nature, and can plainly perceive that there is somewhat more intended than what at first appears in these words of Christ: "No man knoweth the Son, but the Father; neither knoweth any man the Father, but the Son, and to whom the Son will reveal him."* In short, when I contemplate the whole of this awful and mysterious subject, as it is connected with the history of our blessed Lord, and consider the

---

* Matthew xi. 27. Here is a memorable text of Scripture, which, if I mistake not, affords the most decisive determination to the great point in question, and is of itself sufficient to prove the Deity of the Lord Jesus Christ, from the incomprehensibility of his nature. There is a reiteration of the doctrine indeed, and the truth is confirmed in a twofold testimony. If "no man knoweth the Son but the Father;" is not this at once a positive proof that his nature must be infinite which is known only to the infinite mind of God? And could this be said, but upon the fullest evidence, that he of whom it is said is of the same essence with God? But as if this was not enough, the fact is stated again under another form: "neither knoweth any man the Father save the Son, and he to whom the Son will reveal him." Here is, if possible, a still more palpable testimony to the same great truth. For I suppose the incomprehensibility of the divine nature will hardly be questioned; so that by admitting the perfect apprehension of the Father by the Son, while it is hidden, and unknown, to every other being in the universe; nothing can more decidedly prove the Deity of the Son. The reciprocal knowledge of the person, of each other, in the unity of the Godhead, (which is among the distinguishing attributes of GODHEAD, and which, for ever draws the line of separation between the infinite Creator and all created beings whatever;) marks most accurately the great character of each. So very conclusive and satisfactory in point is this single text of Scripture.

But while so much may be gathered from it, by way of carrying conviction to the breast of the unbeliever; it ought not to be passed over and forgotten, what a refreshing consolation it offers at the same time to the sincere follower of Jesus. Though the knowledge both of the Father and of the Son is hidden from all penetration by the mere light of the human understanding; yet where Christ is graciously pleased to afford the knowledge of the Father, every proper apprehension suited to the present condition of man is then given to those humble souls, to whom the Son will reveal him. They know indeed both the Father and the Son, by the power of that grace which they feel in their hearts. They know that Christ is "one with the Father, over all God blessed for ever: being rich unto all that call upon him." And from "the anointing which they have received from him, they need not that any man should teach them;" but can say with the apostle, "truly our fellowship is with the Father, and with his Son Jesus Christ," 1 John i. 3.

the defective state of our present faculties, the very great probability (to say the least of it,) that human beings, after all their researches, will never penetrate very deeply into the secret dispensations of God : I stand amazed that any man should be bold enough to refuse his assent to doctrines because they are not commensurate to reason ; much more that he should deny the divinity of the Son of God upon the presumptive conclusions of his own mind, in opposition to such a body of evidence as is contained in every part of the pure oracles of God. While the argument remains at all doubtful, which the hardest Socinian will scarcely venture to pronounce finished, surely it must be safer to err (if it be an error) on one side than the other; to give too much dignity to the great Saviour of the world, whom the Father delighteth to honour, rather than too little. For the very reason which Christ gives, why the future judgment is committed unto the Son, is on this express account, " that all men should honour the Son, even as they honour the Father ; and he that honoureth not the Son, honoureth not the Father which hath sent him."

But I am anticipating the observations which will come with greater force and propriety hereafter. Let me only hope that enough has now been said to convince your judgment, that *He*, of whom these great things are so confidently said, cannot possibly be a creature. And since common sense revolts at the absurdity of supposing him divine, and yet not God ; I trust we are among the number of those humble and teachable minds, who presume not to reject the testimony of Scripture, because the doctrine of God Incarnate is too mysterious for reason to explore.

SERMON III.

JOHN v. 39.

"*Search the Scriptures,—they are they which testify of me.*"

THE noble faculty of reason, which is the distinguishing excellence of man, among other eminent uses is evidently given him to direct his judgment, and to guard his mind from error and delusion. From the present imperfect state of things, however, reason, unassisted by some superior principle, finds perpetual difficulties, which perplex and confound the understanding. Human nature is always open to imposition. We frequently behold objects through false mediums. We argue from mistaken prinples. We adopt opinions which we afterwards find to be erroneous; and yet too often, from the influence of those prepossessions, we draw our conclusions. Hence, therefore, we cannot be too much upon our guard, how we hastily determine on any matter. After all our most vigilant observations, how little knowledge are we able to obtain even of the most common events of life, which pass in daily review before us! But when the great and awful points of religion are the subject of inquiry; when that sacred mystery hid from ages, the wonder of the universe, and which even angels do not comprehend, but "desire to look into," (1 Peter i. 12,) when this is brought before the mind for discussion, with what caution ought we to decide on a matter so abstruse and difficult! Here surely, if any where, reason finds her weakness and insufficiency, and therefore should gladly implore that divine illumination from above, which is promised in Scripture "to the meek and humble."

In the preceding discourse some observations were made with a view to ascertain the dignity of our Lord. His pre-existence to his advent in the flesh was proved from the authority of Scripture; and this fact was supported by another striking circumstance founded on the same testimony, namely, his being the Creator and Preserver of the universe. Under such great and eternal characters does the Author of the Christian faith appear in those sacred records.

But, on the supposition of the truth of these premises, an observation meets us which demands attention. It is this. If Christ really possessed this existence and glory with his Father before the world, and is the maker and upholder of all things; is it not more than probable that some appearance of him should have been discovered through the many intermediate ages, from the fall of man to his advent in the flesh? For though the incarnation of the Son of God, for reasons unknown to us, was postponed to what is called "the fulness of time," in which all the predictions concerning this illustrious character of the Messiah centered; yet surely it is but reasonable to expect some vestige, at least, of this divine person in the earlier ages of the world, especially as God was pleased occasionally to vouchsafe to his fallen and degraded creatures some manifestaions of his will.

This observation is certainly a very proper one, and claims some regard. And though I cannot conceive a proof of this kind to be necessary, on the supposition that the fact itself of Christ's pre-existence is clearly assured, yet if any traces can be found in the Old Testament, corresponding to the account we find of him in the New, they will, no doubt, mutually illustrate and confirm each other; and altogether serve to place the blessed Redeemer's character in such an exalted point of view, as may help to stengthen our faith in this great article of religion.

And here a subject opens to our investigation, which

may engage the closest study, and will reward the greatest exertions of the most enlightened mind. In searching the sacred volume for the footsteps of him "whose goings forth have been from everlasting," (Micah v. 2.) perhaps it will be found that all the dispensations of God, relating to mankind, from the very first dawn of revelation, have been uniformly and invariably carried on in the person of his divine Son: that he is JEHOVAH, to whom is ascribed the creation of the world; who resided occasionally among men before the fall; whose voice Adam heard in the garden of Eden; who personally appeared to Abraham, and to many others, in the patriarchal ages; spake unto Moses from the flaming bush; went before the children of Israel through the wilderness; descended on Mount Sinai enshrined in glory, and gave the law; and was visible, in a great variety of instances, to that people, as best suited the various purposes of his will. In short, from the creation of the world, to the final consummation of all things, it is he, and he only, who is the visible JEHOVAH, and hath carried on, and will complete, the executive part of the divine government, appearing under the several characters mentioned of him in Scripture, according as the circumstances of mankind required, in the several ages of the world. Hence he is our Creator, Preserver, Redeemer, and finally will be our Judge, when he cometh, agreeable to his promise, at the last day, to close the whole of his government in righteousness; "to be glorified in his saints, and admired in all that believe," (2 Thes. i. 10.)

Now, whether this opinion can derive any countenance and authority from Scripture, is the important question; but it must be confessed there is nothing in it which is foreign to our most natural ideas of the Supreme Being, or repugnant either to reason or revelation. On the contrary, there seems to be an admirable consistency and agreement with both. For that the same divine person who made the world, and by whose energy and power it is continually preserved and supported, should interpose to rectify and amend the evils crept into it by human infirmity, and at length should come to judge the moral subjects of his government, who by their different abilities are placed in a situation of becoming accountable creatures; this is certainly just what might be expected, and corresponding to all our notions of right reason. And, on the supposition that this is the true state of the case, I will venture to say, the mind of man cannot conceive any thing more magnificent and awful, than that of a divine and almighty Being descending from a state of glory, and taking upon him a form of flesh, in order "to repair the desolations of many generations," and to restore perfect order among all the works of God. The whole process of the divine dispensations, according to this scheme, is begun, carried on, and will be completed, by him who "is the same yesterday, to-day, and for ever," (Heb. xiii. 8.)

It cannot be supposed, in the very nature of things, that human faculties are competent to trace so mysterious a subject very far. "The way of God, (says the Psalmist) is in the sea, and his path in the great waters, and his footsteps are not known," (Psalm lxxvii. 19.) Yet as the divine goodness, in order as it were to excite the attention of man, hath graciously condescended to throw some rays of light around the darkness of the scene, and hath moreover promised the assistance of his Holy Spirit to all that, in humility of mind, seek instruction from above; there appears an evident duty, as well as a reward of the noblest kind, attending the investigation of this most interesting of all subjects. And what can engage the attention of the human mind with so much satisfaction, as the humble endeavour to explore the footsteps of that great Benefactor of mankind, to whom we owe such inexpressible obligations? In doing this, we are also obeying the precept which our blessed LORD gave to the Jews, upon a similar occasion, when he referred them to the sacred writings for the evidences of his commission and authority: "Search the Scriptures (says Christ,) for in them ye think ye have eternal life, and they are they which testify of me." In obedience to this command let us direct our attention to this pursuit; and, after having first implored the Holy Spirit to be our guide, let us examine what information we can gather from thence respecting our divine LORD. Perhaps, now "the vail of the Old Testament is done away in Christ, we may" through the divine blessing, "with open face, behold as in a glass the glory of our Lord," (2 Cor. iii. 15, 18.)

The leading object of the present discourse will be to search the Scriptures for any traces of Christ, in the early ages of the world, sufficient to establish our belief of his personal appearance among men.

The invisibility of the Divine Being to mortal eye is well known to be the doctrine of both Testaments of Scripture. "Thou canst not see my face and live," saith Jehovah to Moses. (Ex. xxxiii. 20.) And the apostles of Christ assert the same thing. "No man (saith St. John) hath seen God at any time," (John i. 18.) And St. Paul assures us, "that God dwelleth in that ight which no man can approach unto; whom no man hath seen nor can see," (1 Tim. vi. 16.) He is "the King eternal, immortal, invisible," (1 Tim. i. 17.) And our blessed Lord himself, to sum up the evidence, hath declared, that "no man hath seen the Father, save he which is of God, he hath seen the Father," (John vi. 46.) "Ye have neither heard his voice at any time, nor seen his shape," (John v. 37.) From all which it is evident that the sight of God* is inadmissible to man in his present state.

---

* Here, once for all, I would beg to observe, respecting the glorious name of God, in order for a clear, spiritual, and scriptural apprehension. We are too apt to confine the name to the Person of the FATHER,

This being a fact perfectly incontrovertible, the question is, what are we to understand from those numerous passages of Scripture where the presence of the Lord is most positively assured, unless we apply it to the person of God's only begotten Son, who is declared to be "the brightness of his glory and the express image of his person?" Without referring to all the instances of this kind which might be brought forward in proof, I believe every one who is at all conversant with the sacred writings, will immediately recollect, that there are many very striking passages where the personal appearance of Jehovah is declared to have happened, and upon various occasions. I am not speaking of such as are visional, or figurative, but real and certain. I am sensible of the allowances to be made for the metaphorical language of Scripture, so suited to the genius of the Eastern nations. Thus, the *right arm* of the Lord, and the *voice* of the Lord; these, no doubt are figurative expressions: and earthquakes, storms, and tempests, by way of figure, are sometimes called *angels*, and *messengers* of Jehovah. But this is not the case in the circumstance to which I allude. When, for example, we read in the book of Exodus, "that Jehovah talked with Moses face to face, as a man talketh with his friend," (Exod. xxxiii. 11.) So again, when in a conference like this with the great father of the faithful, Jehovah assumes to himself a supreme

when we find it alone, and unaccompanied with any other of the Persons in the GODHEAD. But this is wrong. All the Persons in the GODHEAD are included; and all are alike meant, except where the Persons of either are personally mentioned. Hence, when it is said, "God was in CHRIST," (2 Cor. v. 19,) all the Persons were and are in CHRIST. So when it is said, (Colos. ii. 9,) "In Him," that is CHRIST, dwelleth all the fulness of the GODHEAD bodily," all are equally included. It would be very helpful, under divine teaching, to keep this always in remembrance, because all approaches to GOD implies FATHER, SON, and HOLY GHOST. Each person in the GODHEAD being alike God; and to whom no approaches can be made to either, but through the mediation of CHRIST. Hence, in respect to the GODHEAD, all are alike invisible. GOD is only seen in CHRIST. By the medium of our nature he is the visible JEHOVAH, (John i. 18.)

power, and speaks of his future dispensations respecting mankind, not as the agent of another, but as acting in his own name, and by his own authority, (Gen. xvii.) And when it is said also, in another place, "that Aaron, Nadab, and Abihu, and seventy of the elders of the people saw the God of Israel," (Exod. xxiv. 9, 10.) These instances surely can never be called visional, symbolical, or figurative. It is plain sense and plain meaning, and if there be any one matter of fact on which we may safely depend, it must be here; for if these repeated assurances of the personal appearance of Jehovah can, by any plausible argument, be reduced to a mere figure or vision, there is nothing to be met with in the whole volume of Scripture but, by a like accommodation, may be as easily construed away from its first and most obvious acceptation.

That all these appearances were in the person of the Son of God, I by no means assert: upon so mysterious a subject I would be understood as speaking with the utmost caution and diffidence. Could the point once be proved that it was our blessed Lord, there would be an end to all controversy respecting his divinity; such manifestations of GODHEAD, accompanied with such declarations of character, must for ever silence all doubts on this head. But if they be real appearances, and not figurative, and if (as an apostle tells us) that though "no man hath seen God at any time, yet the only begotten Son, which is in the bosom of the Father, he hath declared him," (John i. 11,) it seems very likely to suppose that all the accounts we meet with in Scripture of the manifestation of a personal Jehovah, might, with great safety, be explained by this infallible rule.

But, that we may not too hastily determine on this important matter, let us search the word of God further, and see whether we can gain any additional information that may illustrate this point more fully.

One leading principle, to help us in this inquiry, the

Jewish Scriptures happily supply. In the relation they give of this appearance of Jehovah, we find, throughout the whole history, but one and the same being uniformly described. However distinguished by different appellations or titles, as might best correspond to the immediate purpose of his appearing, whether he be called the God of Abraham, Isaac, and Jacob, the God of Israel, or the Angel of the Covenant, still one and the same person is invariably intended. The Jehovah which expelled Adam from the garden of Eden, was the same Jehovah who made a covenant with Abraham, and who declared that "he would not leave him until he had done all that he had spoken to him of, and that in his seed should all families of the earth be blessed," (Gen. xxviii. 15.) Accordingly we find he renewed this covenant with the patriarchs, and again revealed himself to Moses, from the flaming bush, under the same almighty distinctions. And when, from the Egyptian bondage, after a series of the most stupendous events, he had led the children of Israel through the wilderness, until he had brought them into the promised Canaan; upon every occasion in which he was graciously pleased to manifest his presence, the same great character was invariably proclaimed by which he was distinguished as their God, and they his people, and the sheep of his pasture. At length, when the Israelites were settled in their own borders, and a temple was built to the more immediate honour of their Lord, though the personal appearance of Jehovah was now withdrawn, the Shechinah, or manifestation of his glory, still appeared, shadowing the mercy-seat, but without form or similitude; yet before his departure, and when the temple was destroyed, the same Jehovah assured them, by his prophets, that "he would return again in the latter days, and dwell in the midst of them," (Zech. ii. 10;) that "the glory of the latter house should be greater than the former," (Hag. ii. 9;) and that he would make a "new covenant with the house of Israel, aad the house of Judah, not according to the covenant that he had made with their fathers, in the day when he had brought them from the land of Egypt," (Jer. xxxi. 31.) All which evidently and clearly proves, that one and the same Almighty Being constantly presided over the affairs of his church.

This identity of person and character will be of great help to us in our inquiry to whom it belongs. And if we can find a single instance of sufficient authority from the New Testament, to suppose it applicable to our blessed Lord, it will throw a considerable degree of light upon the whole history, and become not a little conclusive to the point in question.

Among many circumstances of this kind, which might be brought forward as presumptive evidences to induce the belief, that the personal Jehovah of the Old Testament is the same being with the Lord of the New, the following are remarkably striking:

When Jehovah appeared to Moses in the flame of fire in the bush, he was pleased to reveal himself under that great and eternal distinction, "I am that I am," (Exod. iii. 14;) which is the very appellation Christ assumed, when, discoursing with the Jews on the subject of his mission, he claimed a priority of existence to Abraham, and said, "Before Abraham was, I am," (John viii. 58;) an argument strongly presumptive, at least, that when our blessed Lord distinguished himself by this incommunicable name of the great Jehovah, he referred to this awful scene, and thereby intimated his real character. And that the Jews considered our Lord's meaning in this sense is more than probable, for they immediately took up stones to cast at him, for the supposed blasphemy; but he, by virtue of this very divinity, in a miraculous manner, so concealed himself from their knowledge, that "going through the midst of them," they knew him not, "and he passed by," (John viii. 59.)

Another instance, very highly presumptive to justify

our belief that our blessed Lord was the very Jehovah mentioned in the Old Testament, we meet with in the writings of the apostle Paul, in which he is illustrating a passage of the Jewish history. The passage is this. The children of Israel, in their journey through the wilderness, pitched in Rephidim, where they murmured for want of water; upon which occasion Moses cried unto the Lord, and the Lord commanded Moses, saying, "Go on before the people, and take with thee of the elders of Israel; and the rod wherewith thou smotest the river take in thine hand, and go. Behold, I will stand before thee there, upon the rock in Horeb, and thou shalt smite the rock, and there shall come water out of it, that the people may drink. And Moses did so in the sight of the elders of Israel."* Now, that no one should be at a loss for the explanation of this passage, we have the authority of an apostle to apply this personal appearance of Jehovah to our blessed Lord. "For they drank," says he, "of that spiritual rock that followed them, and that spiritual rock was Christ."*

Similar to this, upon another occasion, in the history of that people, when Jehovah sent fiery serpents to destroy some for their disobedience and murmuring, the apostle, in his reflections and observations upon their unworthy behaviour, uses this remarkable argument to his Corinthian converts, to deter them from the imitation of so bad an example. "Neither," says he, "let us tempt Christ, as some of them also tempted, and were destroyed of serpents."† A plain proof that it was the opinion of St. Paul that the Jehovah who conducted the Israelites through the wilderness, and manifested himself to them upon various occasions, was no other than Christ.

Lastly; the Evangelist St. John makes an application of a passage in one of the prophets, which seems

* Compare Exodus xvii. with 1 Cor. x.

† Compare Numbers xxi. with 1 Cor. x.

to remove all doubt that the glory of Jehovah, which the prophet beheld in a vision, was the glory of Christ himself. Our blessed Lord having wrought no conviction upon the hearts of his hearers, at a time when preaching his gospel to them, though his doctrine was attested with the operation of miracles, this brought to mind to the apostle the prediction of Isaiah the prophet: "He hath blinded their eyes, and hardened their heart, that they should not see with their eyes, nor understand with their heart and be converted, and I should heal them. These things said Esaias, when he saw his glory, and spake of him."* This quotation from the prophet, which the Evangelist without hesitation applies to Christ, carries with it an evidence not easily refuted. And if the authority of such an expositor is at all valid to our argument, it must, I think, have great weight with every candid mind.†

But these evidences will be strengthened in their importance, when we proceed to consider also certain peculiarities ascribed to the person of Christ by the sacred writers, and assumed by Jesus himself; which could not with the smallest shadow of reason, be applied to him, but under the idea that he was the Jehovah and God of Israel, which appeared to our fathers in the wilderness. St. John, in the first chapter of his gospel, speaking of the eternal Word, "which was in the beginning with God, and was God; who made the world, was in the world, and the world knew him not," adds also, that "he came unto his own, and his own

* Compare Isaiah vi. with John xii.

† It were easy to adduce many instances more than those I have mentioned, but one or two are sufficient for the purpose; some of those I have omitted are very much to the point in question, and have been very largely treated of by other writers. Such as the similarity between the glory of Jehovah in the mount, and our Lord's transfiguration, and which induced those reflections in the mind of the apostle Peter. The appearance of the Captain of the Lord's host to Joshua; the preaching of Christ in the days of Noah, as mentioned by St. Peter, &c. &c.

received him not," (John i.) This is a strong implication of Christ's being relatively known before. For, whether we consider the expression *his own* as referring to the Jews, who were called God's peculiar people, or whether by right, as the Creator of the world; in either case his pre-existence, and personal connection with mankind, by virtue of some priority of right and inheritance, must be pre-supposed and admitted. It could not be in his character, as the Redeemer of the world, for in this case the right would have preceded the purchase; and moreover, this would have made the expression inapplicable to the Jews only. It evidently proves, therefore, some antecedent connection, by virtue of which Christ was their Lord, and they his people. And where are we to look for this but in that history where it is said, "Jehovah chose them to be a special people to himself, above all the people who were upon the face of the earth?" (Deut. vii. 6.)

Again; Christ's lamentation over Jerusalem, and the particular and affecting expressions he made use of upon that occasion, is another very great probability (to speak the least of it) of our Lord's personal appearance and connection with the children of Israel, before his incarnation. St. Luke informs us, that "when he came near to Jerusalem, he beheld the city and wept over it," (Luke xix. 41.;) and St. Matthew, in his account of this transaction, adds, that he brake forth into that tender apostrophe, "O Jerusalem, Jerusalem, thou that killest the prophets, and stonest them that were sent unto thee, how often would I have gathered thy children together, even as a hen gathereth her chickens under her wings, and ye would not!" (Matthew xxiii. 37.) Now it becomes a very proper question, under what part of the sacred history of the life of Jesus Christ do we find this anxiety for Israel, before the season of his humiliation in the flesh? In what page of the Testament are we to look for those repeated instances of his love and solicitude for them? There is no one passage that can, with the smallest propriety, be considered as relating to Christ's passionate lamentation over this unhappy people. It is plain, therefore, that he must have alluded to some former period, when he says, he would often have gathered the children of Israel together, with an anxiety equal to that of the hen, when she seeks to cover her brood from danger, with the spreading of her wings. And corresponding to this idea, we find, in the 31st chapter of Deuteronomy, that Jehovah is represented as exceedingly anxious for the preservation of his people; that "he found them in a desert land, and in the waste howling wilderness; that he led him about and instructed him, and kept him as the apple of his eye. Jéhovah alone did lead him, there was no strange God in him." Now if Jehovah alone did lead him, and Christ, in his anxiety, evidently referred to some former instances of his affection; is it not a most probable conclusion, that this history is altogether applicable to our blessed Lord?

These circumstances are to me, I confess, very strong presumptive evidences at least, that Christ was the visible Jehovah, who occasionally appeared both before, and under the Jewish dispensation. The application made by the sacred writers in the history of Christ to that period; the peculiarities distinguishable in our Lord's person; and the expressions he himself made use of, will hardly admit of any other construction.

But there is another argument, yet remaining to be considered, which gives strength and confirmation to the whole, and is certainly superior to every other; on the truth of which, if I mistake not, depends, in a great measure, the connection of both Testaments of Scripture, and which, indeed if it be not allowed, destroys all consistency between them; and that is, Christ cannot be the Messiah, nor the real lawgiver of Christians, unless he answers to the character predicted of him in the Scriptures of the Jews.

This view of the subject is striking, and deserves a more particular discussion.

I have already observed, in the course of this sermon, that the history of the Jewish church, by preserving an identity of person in the great and almighty Protector of their nation, has happily supplied us with one leading principle to guide us through the mysterious part of our subject. And here it becomes most eminently serviceable. For it is evident, from all the history of that people, that the Jehovah who appeared to Abraham, and made an everlasting covenant with him, and confirmed this covenant to his descendants in the solemn promulgation of the law on Mount Sinai, and continued the manifestation of his presence among that people occasionally, as circumstances required, until the building of the temple; expressly promised, before he withdrew the glory of his appearance, that he would come again in the latter days, and dwell among them. "Sing and rejoice, O daughter of Zion; for, lo, I come, and I will dwell in the midst of thee, saith the Lord," (Zech. ii. 10.) "And in that day it shall be said, Lo, this is our God, we have waited for him, and he will save us: this is the Lord, we have waited for him, we will be glad, and rejoice in his salvation," (Isaiah xxv. 9.) All which plainly refers to one and the same person and character; for in that day it is said, "The Lord shall be king over all the earth; and there shall be one Lord, and his name one." (Zech. xiv. 9.) And as a further confirmation of this, the prophet Jeremiah expressly declares, that the Jehovah who made the old covenant with the house of Israel and the house of Judah, is the same Jehovah who would return again in the latter days, and make a new one. "Behold, the days come, saith the Lord, that I will make a new covenant with the house of Israel, and the house of Judah; not according to the covenant that I made with their fathers, in the day that I took them by the hand, to bring them out of the land of Egypt; which my covenant they brake, although I was an husband to them, saith the Lord; but this shall be the covenant that I will make with the house of Israel; After those days, saith the Lord, I will put my law in their inward parts, and write it in their hearts; and I will be their God, and they shall be my people," (Jer. xxxi. 31, 32.)

Now from the testimony of these Scriptures we have authority to draw the following conclusions: first, That the same Almighty Jehovah which led, and governed, and protected the children of Israel, during the whole of their eventful history, was expected to come again and dwell among them in the latter days: and, secondly, that this Jehovah at his return, was to make a new covenant with the house of Israel, and the house of Judah, and different from the covenant which he had before made with their fathers, in the day he took them by the hand, to bring them out of the land of Egypt. Hence, therefore, it seems to follow, that if Christ be not the Jehovah which manifested himself to the Israelites in the wilderness, according to those scriptures he is not the Jehovah they were taught to expect, and consequently, not the Messiah. Neither could he be the Jehovah which was to make a *new* covenant with the house of Israel, unless he be the same Jehovah which made the *old*.

And this identity of person and character, is not only essential to be preserved for the completion of these promises of Scripture, but must be carefully distinguished on another equally important consideration. The Jews were plainly taught to expect a change in their system of legislation, but they were as plainly taught it should be accomplished by one and the same being. The Jehovah which was to make the new covenant, was the founder of the old; and nothing less than this could certainly be sufficient for its alteration: for as the law given on Mount Sinai was of divine authority, and accompanied with all the manifestations of the divine presence, it is evident none but the original law-giver himself could possibly supersede, or do away its obligation. Nor was this change in the law of Moses the smallest impeachment of the immutability of the divine nature. For the alteration was not in God, but man. The *moral* law still continues the same, and will remain for ever; for it is of eternal duration: and as Christ observed, "Sooner might heaven and earth pass than one jot or tittle of this law to fail. He came," therefore, "not to destroy this law, but to fulfil it." But the *ceremonial* law could be no longer necessary, when the purpose for which it ministered was answered and completed; when the substance was once come, the shadow was, of course, done away. Besides, many reasons concurred also to render the removal of the Mosaic ordinances expedient. When the Israelites became scattered into divers countries, there could no longer remain the possibility of performing the sacrifices at the Temple, nor of appearing three times in a year at their solemn feasts at Jerusalem. And when the kingdom of the Messiah was come, which by a progressive influence was to extend over the whole earth, the name of Jehovah, no longer limited to an handful of people, was to be "great among the Gentiles, and in every place incense was to be offered unto his name, and a pure offering."

From these united considerations it appears to be a fair and probable conclusion, that the great lawgiver of Christians is the original lawgiver of the Jews; for this preserves an harmony (which otherwise is broken) between both Testaments of Scripture, and proves them to be consistent with the divine immutability on which the whole is founded.

If then these circumstances, collectively taken from

a body of evidence sufficient to rest our belief on, that the great Author of the Christian faith, whose dignity and character we have in part already reviewed, who was in possession, as he himself assures us, of "glory with the Father before the world was," and whom the sacred writers declare to have been in conjunction with his Father, the *Maker* and *Preserver* of *all things;* if the circumstances, I say, collectively taken, authorize our belief that Jesus is the Jehovah who personally appeared under the Jewish dispensation, and in the earlier ages of the world, I think it will follow, that every objection to his divinity must yield to the clear and express revelation of his having appeared among men previous to his incarnation; and we have reason to believe, that all the ordinations of God respecting mankind, have been uniformly and invariably conducted in the person of his blessed Son.

Though what hath been now offered cannot, from the very nature of things, be considered more than the faint outlines of a subject, which taken in all its parts, surpasses human ability to explore; yet I should hope it is sufficient to give some little insight (as far as we have Scripture authority to carry us) into this part of the mysterious government of God. And from this view we not only perceive a wonderful consistency throughout the whole design of revelation, but also the conclusion naturally resulting from it; namely, that one and the same Almighty Architect both planned and executed the physical and moral structure of our nature.

And now I should hope, the evidence for the GODHEAD of Jesus, like a mighty river, increasing as it descends from the numerous streams pouring into it on every side, swells upon your mind and carries all opposition before it. And when we come to view the testimonies which appear in the history of our blessed Lord during his incarnation, all leading to the same conclusion, our hearts, overpowered with the torrent of conviction, will cry out with Nathaniel, "This is the Son of God, this is the King of Israel."

SERMON IV.

ACTS XXVIII. 23.

Persuading them concerning Jesus, both out of the law of Moses, and out of the Prophets.

ONE of the decisive and infallible evidences of the Christian religion is derived from the Scriptures of the prophets. The wonderful circumstances relating to the future kingdom of the Messiah, are described by one or other of those holy men of God, with such precision and particularity, as cannot but fill the mind with astonishment, when we discover the prediction and the event bearing the most minute correspondence. Delivered in ages remote from the time of completion, and the subject of their prophecy being altogether improbable, according to all human ideas, we cannot suppose it to arise from any effects of foresight or penetration. Nor can it be said, with any colour of reason, that the prediction was written after the accomplishment of the event. It is only to be accounted for, as proceeding from the powerful and immediate inspiration of Almighty God; and as such, therefore, it stamps, with the strongest seal of truth, the cause to which it is intended to bear evidence, for "the testimony of Jesus is the spirit of prophecy," Revelation xix. 10.

If we look into these inspired writings with a view to answer the more immediate object of our present pursuit, the great question will be, under what character the Jews were taught by their prophets to expect their promised Messiah, and what were to be the specific marks of his person and offices?

It may well be supposed the appearance of such an august Being upon the theatre of this world, and who was coming on that grand embassy, to save and restore a fallen race, must have had some most striking and prominent features by which he might be known. If the divine Saviour thought the object important enough to typify and predict it through a long course of ages; it is but reasonable to suppose also, that those types and prophecies must have particularly shadowed the outlines of his person and character.

Let us search the sacred records once more for information on this point, and see what were the individual characters which the Scriptures of the prophets taught mankind to look for in the great Saviour of the world.

It is well known, and therefore needless to be insisted on in this place, that the prospect of a Messiah was the leading principle of the Jewish religion. Through the many intermediate ages from the promise of this deliverer, to the period of his appearance, the minds of men were continually occupied with the expectation of this auspicious event. Every thing ceremonial in the service of the Jews was, for the most part, typical or figurative of it. I pass over the general features by which the Messiah was described, and by which Jesus of Nazareth identified his claim to that character. Neither the precise time of his appearance, nor the circumstances by which that appearance was to be distinguished and known, as answering to the spirit of prophecy, are immediate to my present purpose. In this point all Christians of every denomination are agreed, and it is needless, therefore, to dwell upon them. The great and only object now in view is, to ascertain, if possible, what was to be the real character of the promised Messiah, according to the language of prophecy; and I shall have no further recourse to the Scriptures of the prophets, than as they tend to the illustration of this important article.

Among the writings of those inspired men, we find the Messiah so minutely described, under one or other of his offices, that an attentive mind cannot help being struck when he beholds the wonderful vein of prophecy which runs through the whole of their works. Some of them so very plain and obvious, that even an ordinary reader, who considers them in a prophetic sense, must be instantly led to make application of them to the person of our blessed Lord. Others, indeed, are rather hidden and obscure, and such as we should not have been able, with any precision or certainty, to have known Christ by, if the apostles, in their expositions of those Scriptures, under the assistance of the Spirit of God, had not pointed out their allusion. Those who have leisure and ability to go through the whole of the prophecies on this important subject, will find enough to excite their admiration, and confirm their conviction; but I am necessarily limited to selections only. And of these the first place is due, in priority of time, to the predictions of the royal prophet David.

He speaks of Christ, in his Book of Psalms, under so many and various particulars of his incarnation, his sufferings, his death, and exaltation at the right hand of power, that it would extend the subject much beyond what I propose, to bring before you every prediction we meet with in his writings, which hath a clear reference to the person of our Lord.

If the second Psalm can be supposed to have any prophetic meaning, nothing can be more to the purpose in proof of the divinity of him to whom it is applicable. The anointed of the Lord is there said to be "the King of Zion," and "the Son of God," whose inheritance was to be "over the heathen," and his possessions to extend "to all the kingdoms of the world." Similar to this in the 89th Psalm, we find the same person predicted under the title of "the Holy One," and "one that is mighty," and declared to be God's "firstborn, higher than the kings of the earth." And that these things were not spoken of David himself, but as a type of the Messiah, is evident, both from the expressions made use of, and the characters by which he is distinguished. For David, in his highest glory, could not be called the "Holy One," and the "mighty." Nor could he possibly possess those properties ascribed to the King of Zion. Nor did the ancient Jews, indeed, ever consider them as applicable to any but their expected deliverer. But had we any doubts remaining to whom they referred, the apostles Paul and John would remove them; for the one calls Christ the "first-born of every creature," (Coloss. i. 15,) and the other "King of kings, and Lord of lords," Rev. xix. 16.

The children singing songs of triumph before our Lord at his entrance into Jerusalem, which the Psalmist predicted, (Psalm viii.;) his persecutions by the princes of the earth, (Psalm ii. and lxix.;) the reproaches and sufferings sustained by his sacred person; the circumstances which attended his crucifixion; the soldiers piercing his side; the parting his garments, and casting lots for his vesture; nay, the very words our Lord used in those trying moments, (Psalm xxii.)—all these particulars, and many more to the same purpose,* which we find in the writings of this prophet, and which are either by our Lord himself, or his apostles, declared to refer to him, clearly imply a superiority of *his* nature whom they predicted.

But, above all, the resurrection of Jesus from the dead, his ascension into heaven, and his possession of an eternal throne at the right hand of power; these are such predictions as, when explained by the corresponding events, can leave no room to doubt the GODHEAD of that person to whom they referred, and in whom they are all accomplished. When we hear, therefore,

* See 110th Psalm, and compare the 40th with the 10th chap. of Hebrews.

the royal prophet declaring the impossibility of the Messiah's seeing *corruption*, and find the apostle Peter applying this prophecy so expressly to Christ, in his first sermon after the descent of the Holy Ghost;* when again we read the magnificent description the prophet hath given of his "ascending up on high, leading captivity captive, and receiving gifts for men;" and see the whole verified in the day of our Lord's ascension, and his sending down the gifts of his Holy Spirit on his followers at the feast of Pentecost; † and when the prophet says of him, "Thy throne, O God, is for ever and ever, the sceptre of thy kingdom is a right sceptre;" and behold the very words quoted by an infallible expositor that cannot be mistaken, and without hesitation applied to him whom he calls "God's eternal Son, the brightness of his glory, and the express image of his person:"‡ I would ask any candid and ingenuous mind, what possible ideas we can annex to such qualities but those which are divine? and therefore, what less than a divine being could the prophet have meant to predict in the promised Messiah?

From David let us pass on to Isaiah, who, from the great variety of events, as well as the striking particulars he hath spoken of, when sketching the outlines of the Messiah's character, is, by way of eminence, distinguished by the title of the Evangelical Prophet. Such, indeed, are the writings of this wonderful man on the subject of Christ's person and offices, that the most striking scenes of our Lord's passion are delineated by the prophet's pencil, with the same truth and exactness as if they had been drawn on the spot, when the secret volume of the divine decrees was unrolled, and when that which had been foreseen in vision was exhibited in reality.

The prophet begins his description of the person of

* I stay not to quote the passages; compare Psalm xvi. with Acts ii.

† Compare Psalm lxviii. with Ephesians iv.

‡ Compare Psalm xlv. with Hebrews i.

the future Messiah with the nicest discrimination of character, when predicting his miraculous conception. "Behold (says he) a virgin shall conceive and bear a son, and shall call his name Emmanuel." An angel hath testified the application of this prophecy in the person of Jesus, and an apostle hath recorded the fact itself of its being accomplished: "All this was done, that it might be fulfilled which was spoken of the Lord by the prophets."*

In another chapter Isaiah again foretels the birth of the Messiah, and with such additional marks of divinity which he ascribes to him, as impress the mind with the fullest conviction of the greatness of his character to whom they belong. "Unto us (says he) a child is born, unto us a Son is given, and the government shall be upon his shoulder, and his name shall be called Wonderful; Counsellor; The Mighty God; The Everlasting Father; The Prince of Peace. Of the increase of his government and peace there shall be no end," (Isaiah ix. 6.) What a cluster of attributes and titles of divinity is here! Although I believe there is not a single perfection belonging to the Father, but what in one part or other of sacred Scripture is equally applied to the Son, yet in this verse the incommunicable characters of GODHEAD shine out like a full constellation. The inspired writer appears to want words to denote "the fulness of him who filleth all in all," (Ephes. i. 23.) How could the prophet be so daring and presumptuous as to describe the Messiah under such great and eternal properties, if, after all, no more than a mere man was expected in him? Would he have said this of any, even of the highest and greatest of all created beings? Could such attributes, in the smallest degree, be applicable to any less than the Great Supreme? and what then were the expectations of the Jews, from the predictions of Isaiah, of the character of their Messiah?

* Compare Isaiah vii. 14, with Matthew i. 22.

The same prophet, after having enumerated those wonderful properties of the nature of the Messiah, goes on to mention other particulars, descriptive of his person and character. He foretells the herald which should usher in his approach, the name and title by which he should be proclaimed, the manner of his appearance, and the great events by which his life would be distinguished. "The voice of one crying in the wilderness, Prepare ye the way of the Lord, make straight in the desert an highway for our God." "Lift up thy voice, be not afraid; say unto the cities of Judah, Behold your God!" (Isaiah xl. 3, 9.) "Behold, your God will come and save you. Then the eyes of the blind shall be opened, and the ears of the deaf shall be unstopped; then shall the lame man leap as an hart, and the tongue of the dumb shall sing."* Observe these expressions, I beseech you, and then turn to the evangelist's history of the life of Jesus, and behold the correspondence of the prediction with the event! Recollect what the prophet hath said, that it was *their God* who was to come and save them, "when the eyes of the blind were opened, and the ears of the deaf unstopped;" and then view the blessed Redeemer of mankind going about the streets of Jerusalem, continually performing those gracious works of mercy, and referring the messengers of John the Baptist to those very actions, as proofs that he was the character predicted; and then determine what stronger proofs can be required of the divinity of his person, in whom all these properties were united.

Nor will the predictions of the other prophets concerning the Messiah be found less expressive of his nature and dignity, though they are not so diffuse and particular as those of David or Isaiah.

What less than a Divine Being did Jeremiah teach the Jews to look for in their expected deliverer, when he declared the name by which he should be known was

* Compare Isaiah xxxv. 5, 6. with Matthew xi. 2—6

the incommunicable name of the great Jehovah? "This is the name (says he) whereby he shall be called, The Lord our righteousness," (Jer. xxiii. 6.) What character could the prophet Daniel expect he was to appear in, whom he describes as the "Son of Man coming in the clouds of heaven; and to whom there was given dominion, and glory, and a kingdom; and whom all people and nations should serve, whose dominion was to be an everlasting dominion?"*

This prophet also, in a very particular manner, declares the precise time of the Messiah's appearing, and of his being cut off, together with the great end of his sacrificial merits and death; all which were literally fulfilled, according to his predictions, in the person of Christ: but I mention these things only as additional proofs, to whom the prophet evidently referred from those corresponding circumstances.

The prophet Micah hath so clearly defined the person and character of our Lord, in that memorable prophecy which points to the very spot which was to give birth to the Redeemer, that no one who admits the prediction to have a reference to Jesus Christ, can hesitate in believing also that it ascribes deity to him whom it predicted. "Thou, Bethlehem Ephratah, though thou be little among the thousands of Judah, yet out of thee shall he come forth unto me that is to be ruler in Israel, whose goings forth have been from of old, from everlasting," (Micah v. 2.) If this passage can be supposed to have reference to the expected Messiah, and we have the testimony of the Scriptures in full proof of this opinion, (Matt. ii. 5, 6.; John vii. 42,) it plainly follows, that this Messiah, whom the Jews were taught to look for, was a being possessed of an eternal nature, "whose goings forth have been from of old, from everlasting."

And if Haggai means any thing by that remarkable prophecy, that the glory of the latter house shall be

* Compare Daniel vii. 13, 14, with Matt. xxiv. 30.

greater than of the former, (Haggai ii. 6—9,) it could only be derived from the divinity of *his* presence, who appeared in it during his incarnation: for we read in Scripture, that the second temple was so far inferior to the first, that many of the priests and chief of the fathers, who were ancient men, that had seen the first house, when the foundation of the second was laid before their eyes, "wept with a loud voice."*

But Zechariah hath yet more particularly defined the character of the expected Messiah, by the Spirit of prophecy with which he wrote, when he says, "Sing and rejoice, O daughter of Zion: for, lo, I come, and I will dwell in the midst of thee, saith the Lord. And many nations shall be joined to the Lord in that day, and shall be my people; and thou shalt know that the Lord of hosts hath sent me unto thee," (Zech. ii. 10, 11.) Here are evidently very discriminating marks by which the Messiah's character should be ascertained. He is called the *Lord*, and said to be sent by the *Lord of hosts*: by which the incommunicable name of Jehovah is equally applied both to the Father and to the Son. And to express this still more, in a subsequent part of his prophecy, he uses this remarkable language: "Awake, O sword, against my shepherd, and against the man that is my fellow, saith the Lord of hosts; smite the shepherd, and the sheep shall be scattered." Our Lord himself hath so clearly explained this prophecy, that the sense and application of it cannot be doubted. And

* Ezra ii. 12. The Jews have themselves observed five distinguishing excellencies in the first temple, which the second wanted; namely, 1st. The Urim and Thummim, by which the high priest received instructions in the will of God. 2dly. The ark of the covenant, from whence the voice of the Lord was heard. 3dly. The fire upon the altar, which came down from heaven and consumed the sacrifice. 4thly. The divine presence, manifested by a shining glory; and 5thly. The Spirit of prophecy. And, added to these, as the building of the *second* temple, in point of ornament and structure was, in the eyes of the people, as nothing in comparison with the *first*; how was the divine promise completed by filling this house with glory, according to the prophecy of Haggai, unless by the visible appearance of Him to whom it was dedicated?

what then shall we conclude his nature to have been, who is called *fellow to the Lord of hosts?**

I will detain you with but one quotation more from the predictions of the prophets on this subject, and that is of Malachi, who lived about three hundred and fifty years before Christ's advent, and with whose prophecy the sacred volume of the Old Testament closes. "Behold, (says he) I will send my messenger, and he shall prepare the way before me, and the Lord whom ye seek shall suddenly come to HIS temple, even the messenger of the covenant whom ye delight in; behold, he shall come, saith the Lord of hosts."† That this prophecy refers to the person of our Lord, and his harbinger John the Baptist, will not, I believe, be doubted. The question, then, arising from hence is, what less than a divine being were the Jews taught to look for, in one whose way his forerunner proclaimed to be "the way of the Lord;" and who, when he came, was to come as "the Lord to his temple?" How should it be called *his* temple unless he were the Lord of it; and to whom but God himself could a temple be dedicated?

Now, then, review these evidences, arising from the predictions of the prophets, coolly and impartially, and then say under what character the great Deliverer of Israel was to appear. If language may be at all depended upon, and the Holy Spirit which guided the prophet's pen be supposed free from error, no one truth can be more clearly revealed, nor any one fact more fully assured to us, than that the possession of divine attributes was to be the distinguishing feature of his nature and person. And how any man in the face of those Scriptures, can be presumptuous enough decidedly to assert, that the Jews never looked for, nor were they taught to expect, any other than a man like themselves in their Messiah, is incredible indeed!

---

* Compare Zechariah xiii. 7, with Matt. xxvi. 31, and Mark xiv. 27.

† Compare Malachi iii. 1, with Matt. iii. 1, *et seq.*

But though the prophets predicted the future Saviour under those great and eternal distinctions which could only belong to a divine Being, yet, they as expressly described certain characters and qualities at the same time, by which he should be known, and which as evidently demonstrated an human nature.

Though it was said of him, that he should be a Prince which should reign over all, and of his kingdom there shall be no end ; though the Gentiles were to come to his light, and kings to the brightness of his rising ; yet no less was this desire of all nations, this Lord of his temple, to be a man of sorrows, and acquainted with grief ; he was to pour out his soul unto death ; he was to give his back to the smiters, and his cheeks to them that plucked off the hair. When we saw him, there was nothing that we should desire him, his visage was so marred more than any man, and his form more than the sons of men. He was to be wounded for our transgressions, and bruised for our iniquities ; to be led as a lamb to the slaughter ; to be taken from prison, and from judgment ; and to be cut off out of the land of the living.

Predictions so seemingly contradictory in one and the same character, required somewhat more than human comprehension to unravel, before the events foretold were accomplished. Accordingly, the ancient Jews, unable to reconcile them, universally rejected the idea of a suffering Messiah, and fondly embraced that which flattered their notions of worldly greatness, by looking for a triumphant Saviour. But their ignorance and perpetual perversion of the Scriptures do not prevent more enlightened and dispassionate minds (and especially when enabled to judge from the events now in a great measure fulfilled) from seeing things in a different point of view. We perceive in those Scriptures clear and manifest declarations of the union of two distinct characters in one and the same person. The Messiah was evidently to be " Emmanuel, God with us," and no less a "man of sorrows, and acquainted with grief." And well might the prophet, wrapt in the contemplation of so mysterious a character, declare his name should be called "Wonderful;" for, beheld in any light, either as God or man, or as God and man, he is altogether wonderful.

I have dwelt so largely in reciting the quotations from the prophets, to shew the specific marks of the *divine* nature by which the Messiah, it was said, should be distinguished, that I cannot trespass longer upon your time in more particularly selecting those which describe him under his manhood. On this point, indeed, it is less necessary to enlarge. They who differ from us in opinion respecting the divinity of our Lord, will not require proofs, I believe, of his humanity. I would only beg it may be remembered, therefore, that we are equally anxious with them to preserve the belief of Christ's human nature, as the doctrine of Scripture, and an essential article of salvation. While we glory in the gracious plan of redemption by Christ, that the Lord laid help "upon one that is mighty," and sent his Son "to be the Saviour of the world;" it is the peculiar joy also, and consolation of our hearts, that this blessed Redeemer, when he came upon this beneficent errand, "took not upon him the nature of angels, but was made like unto us in all things, yet without sin, that he might be a merciful and faithful high priest in things pertaining to God, to make reconciliation for the sins of the people," (Heb. ii. 16 and iv. 15.)

I have now finished the single object proposed in this discourse, having selected a few of the most striking passages from the prophets (and I hope sufficient to the purpose), to shew what were the leading characters their Scriptures taught mankind to expect in the promised Messiah. And from these premises the fair conclusion deducible is obvious. As those unerring oracles of holy writ, penned under the immediate inspiration of God, have very clearly revealed, that an unity of nature, divine and human, should constitute the expected Redeemer; if Jesus Christ be no more than man, he answers not to this prediction, and consequently is not the true Messiah. But if, in the person of our Lord, we evidently trace marks of this mysterious union, then have we confidence to conclude that he is the promised Saviour, "to whom give all the prophets witness," (Acts x. 43.)

With these discriminating characters in view, let us now direct our inquiry unto the gospel; and, under the gracious assistance of that blessed Spirit whom we humbly trust hath hitherto guided our researches, and will accompany our future progress through this subject; let us examine, and with the most scrupulous exactness, whether our Lord brought with him those infallible marks by which his claims to the person and offices of the Messiah should be ascertained and known.—But this, with divine permission, must be the subject of the next discourse.

SERMON V.

JOHN i. 14.

And the Word was made flesh, and dwelt among us, (and we beheld his glory, the glory as of the only begotten of the Father,) full of grace and truth.

IN the prosecution of the important subject which hath requested your attention, I come now to those manifestations of GODHEAD which distinguished the person of Jesus during his incarnation.

The result of our inquiry in the preceding discourse, concerning the testimony of the prophets in their predictions of the Messiah, was found to be altogether descriptive of a great, but humble Saviour. Though it was the "God of Israel" that was to come and save them, when "the eyes of the blind were to be opened, and the tongue of the dumb to sing," (Isaiah xxxv. 4, 5, 6;) yet was he to be at the same time "a man of sorrows and acquainted with grief," (Isaiah liii.) Though the "Gentiles were to come to his light, and kings to the brightness of his rising," (Isaiah lx. 3.;) yet it was said of him, with no less truth, that "he should give his back to the smiters, and his cheeks to them that plucked off the hair, and hide not his face from shame and spitting," Isaiah l. 6. This enigmatical prophecy, so apparently irreconcilable to the apprehensions of the human mind, was nevertheless literally fulfilled when Christ appeared upon the earth.

The mysterious union of our Lord's two natures, which the Evangelist declares in the words of the text, fully reconciles the seeming contradiction. Hence his description of the person of Jesus. After having ascribed to him all the great and distinguishing characters of divinity; that he was "the Word which was from the beginning with God, and was God; that all things were made by him, and without him was not any thing made which was made," (John i. 1, 2, 3;) he next subjoins the testimony of his incarnation: "the Word was made flesh, and dwelt among us; and we beheld his glory; the glory as of the only begotten of the Father, full of grace and truth."

With this description of the Messiah in our hand, we are now to enter upon that era, in which our blessed Lord made his appearance, when the minds of men were raised to the highest pitch in expectation of the coming Saviour.

The first object of my present discourse will be to examine (as was proposed) what correspondence the character of Jesus bears to the promised prediction, and whether our Lord brought with him those *criteria* by which the Messiah should be known.

At this season (the precise time the prophets had foretold) the angel Gabriel was sent to the city of Nazareth, to announce to a virgin called Mary, tidings of the miraculous conception: thus confirming and illustrating the remarkable prophecy of Isaiah, "Behold, a virgin shall conceive and bear a son, and shall call his name Immanuel," God with us, Isaiah vii. 14.

The particulars of this wonderful embassy are thus related by the Evangelist: "And the angel came in unto her, and said, Hail, thou that art highly favoured, the Lord is with thee; blessed art thou among women. And when she saw him she was troubled at his saying, and cast in her mind what manner of salutation this should be. And the angel said unto her, Fear not, Mary, for thou hast found favour with God: and behold thou shalt conceive in thy womb, and bring forth a son, and shalt call his name JESUS. He shall be great, and shall be called the Son of the Highest; and the Lord God shall give unto him the throne of his father David; and he shall reign over the house of Jacob for ever; and of his kingdom there shall be no end. Then said Mary unto the angel, How shall this be, seeing I know not a man? And the angel answered, and said unto her, The Holy Ghost shall come upon thee, and the power of the Highest shall overshadow thee; therefore, also, that holy thing which shall be born of thee shall be called the Son of God. And Mary said, Behold the handmaid of the Lord, be it unto me according to thy word. And the angel departed from her," Luke i. 28—38. An event of so singular a nature requires somewhat more than ordinary proof to procure the conviction and belief of mankind. It is not by the testimony of the virgin herself, nor even the authority of the sacred historian, (though coming with all the evidences of divine inspiration) alone considered, that we can expect an hearty assent from the pride of the human understanding. There must be somewhat more than these to satisfy scrupulous minds. But when we find concurrent circumstances, and in such instances as defeat all suspicions of collusion or deceit; the correspondence of ancient prophecy with the accomplishment of the fact itself; the message of an angel, attested by the Spirit of God guiding the pen of the evangelist, and the whole illustrated by all the subsequent acts of the Redeemer's life; surely there ought to be no hesitation, with all modest and impartial persons, in receiving the truth of the miraculous conception as an article of religious belief.

As this, however, is so very important a point, in ascertaining the real dignity and character of our blessed Lord, and will best help us to form a true idea of the wonderful events with which his ministry was distinguished; you will not think it foreign to my present purpose, if I enter somewhat more particularly into the evidences of the miraculous conception.

The first circumstance worthy observation in proof of it, ariseth from the prediction of ancient prophecy. It was the express language of the prophet Isaiah, when predicting the advent of the Messiah, that he should be born of a virgin. "A virgin shall conceive and bear a son;"* which words evidently implied a miraculous conception, even if the evangelist, who declares the incarnation of Jesus, had not noticed it. And that no possible misapprehension might arise from the application of this prophecy to the person of our Lord, we find that not only an angel was sent to the Virgin, to give her notice of this supernatural impregnation; but also a visional intimation was delivered to Joseph, her intended husband, in a dream, applying this very passage of the prophecy to the case of the Virgin, and declaring that "all this was done, that it might be fulfilled which was spoken of the Lord by the prophet," (Matthew i. 22.)

The second proof of the miraculous conception is the testimony of the sacred historian, who hath so circumstantially related it. The evangelist, St. Luke, independently of his inspired authority, deserves our attention the more from several weighty particulars with which he has prefaced his narration. He wrote the gospel, he says, purposely because he had a more "perfect understanding of all things from the very first," (relating to the person and ministry of Jesus Christ;) "and forasmuch as many had taken in hand to set forth in order a declaration of those things which were most surely believed among them, even those who were eyewitnesses and ministers of the word, it seemed good to him also to write of the same," (Luke i. 1, 4.) And in this very chapter, in which he hath related the circumstances of the wonderful conception of Mary, he speaks of ano-

* Compare Isaiah vii. 14, with Luke i. 35, and Matt. i. 22.

ther angelic embassy to Zacharias, together with the event and completion of that mission: all which, had any of the facts mentioned been thought questionable, would have invalidated the rest, and rendered the whole history liable to contradiction; and the more so, as this is the first instance upon record of an immediate revelation, for more than three hundred years from the time the spirit of prophecy ceased with the last of the prophets, Malachi. So that in the relation of this sacred writer we have the strongest human testimony to prove the correspondence of the fact itself with the thing predicted.*

But, thirdly, The miraculous conception of Jesus derives its certainty, not only from the prediction of prophecy, and the corresponding event assured to us in the testimony of the sacred historian, but the necessity of the thing itself implies it, in order that Christ might answer the great end of his mission and character.

Notwithstanding some professors of Christianity are so exceedingly anxious to strip the gospel of its principal doctrine of atonement through the blood of Jesus; yet nothing can be more plain and evident than that the prophets, in their declarations of the future Saviour, foretold of a *suffering* Messiah, who should make his soul "an offering for sin," who was to be "wounded for our transgressions and bruised for our iniquities; by whose stripes we should be healed, and on whom the Lord would lay the iniquity of us all," (Isaiah liii.) That when "the weeks were determined to anoint the Most Holy, and to bring in everlasting righteousness, the Messiah should be cut off, but not for himself," (Dan. ix. 24, *et seq.*) These plain predictions of the great

* I beg the reader to observe, that I have taken no notice of the *inspiration* with which the evangelist wrote his gospel, for on this supposition, all further argument would be unnecessary. I am now considering the evidence of his authority simply as an historian writing of a matter of fact, and even from hence I conceive the supernatural birth of our Lord to be fully proved.

objects to be accomplished by the sacrificial merits, and death of the Messiah, loudly proclaimed the expediency of a miraculous conception; for had this not been the case; had our Lord been born by the ordinary course of things, in consequence of Mary's marriage with her husband, partaking then of the common nature, which wa universally corrupt and fallen, the offering of himself as a pure and unblemished sacrifice for sin, would have been impossible; and hence the character of Christ, according to the predictions of the prophets, would have been defective in one of the most important offices of the Messiah: whereas, now, the sufferings and death of Jesus, so exactly corresponding to the Spirit of prophecy, become an additional evidence of our Lord's wonderful incarnation, and both confirm and illustrate each other.

But, lastly, What gives the finishing proof of the miraculous conception, is the wonderful events which followed in the Redeemer's life; for upon no other consideration can we reconcile many of the actions displayed by our Lord, but upon the supposition that he derived his being in a way different from the ordinary means of generation among men.

It would be a digression, in some sort, from the main object now before us, to enter into the detail of those actions of Christ, in order to establish this doctrine. And, indeed, the observations I have to make on them will more properly meet us in another part of this discourse, when I come to prove the GODHEAD of Jesus from his illustrious deeds, which every where proclaimed it. But all I would wish to remark at present is this; that when we find the account of the evangelist of the supernatural pregnancy of Mary, so minutely verifying the predictions of the prophets concerning the birth of the Messiah; and, again, this very circumstance leading to the accomplishment of an event, foretold as one of the distinguishing offices of the Messiah, by which alone the promised Saviour could become a proper sacrifice for sin; and, lastly, when we behold, in the subsequent acts of our Lord's life, such a series of conduct as clearly and decidedly prove a nature superior to every former prophet or teacher; it is but reasonable to conclude, that his birth must have been miraculous, which was produced from the overshadowing power of the Highest, and evidently without the intervention of an human father.

Nor is there any thing incredible in the thing itself to those who will admit, what the angel declared to be the case, the interposition of divine energy in the operation of the Holy Ghost. And the very idea of a miracle pre-supposes this agency. Let us imagine only, what the most presumptuous sceptic cannot deny, that the same great power which created the first man from nothing, and breathed into his nostrils the breath of life, possesses the same ability to produce another man, without the natural means he hath appointed for the continuation of the species: on this supposition it will not appear more surprising that Christ should be born of a virgin, without an human father, than that Adam should be at first formed out of the dust of the ground. In both cases it is the exertion of a supernatural agency; and the very embassy of an angel, in the case of Mary's conception, implied some very important purpose, wherefore this singular event was to be accomplished. Those who are not already converts to the atheistical creed of the world's eternity, or ready to join the scoffers the apostle speaks of, who deride the promise of Christ's future coming to judgment, because they conceive "all things to continue as they were from the beginning of the creation," (2 Peter iii. 4,) must admit there was a time when man began to be: the birth of Jesus, therefore, is not the first instance of an immediate existence without the usual means.

Such are the evidences of the incarnation of our Lord; and I hope they will appear sufficiently conclusive and satisfactory, to establish your hearts in the firm belief of this fundamental principle of the gospel, on the truth of which depend those important doctrines which peculiarly distinguish the Christian religion. Give up this article of your creed; say that Jesus is the son of Joseph, and you give up with it, at once, all the hopes of true believers. Then the great doctrine of atonement, and the cross of Christ, fall to the ground. That cross, which the apostle Paul so much gloried in, (Gal. vi. 14,) and concerning which he "determined to know nothing" beside, (1 Cor. ii. 2:) that cross which is the very seal and badge of our profession: that cross is rendered trifling and nugatory; "our faith is vain, we are yet in our sins," (Cor. xv. 17.)

It is not paying Christ the officious empty compliment that he was the greatest of all teachers and of prophets; this is but a poor recompence for robbing him of his most endearing character, the Redeemer of the world. That Christ was a teacher, come from God, and infinitely surpassing all that were before him, is too plain to be denied. We feel conviction of the divinity of his religion, by the purity of his doctrine. But, were these all the ends the Son of God came upon earth to accomplish, wretched would be still the hopes of fallen man. What more eminently recommends his gospel to our hearts, is the provision it makes for the most material wants of our nature, in "redemption through his blood, even the forgiveness of sins," (Ephes. i. 7;) that he "made our peace through the blood of his cross," (Coloss. i. 20:) and that "if any man sin we have an advocate with the Father, Jesus Christ the righteous, and he is the propitiation for our sins," (1 John ii. 1, 2.) These are the grand and essential points in our holy faith, and therefore let me beg of you, in terms equal to their importance, to pray for grace that you may remain firm and unshaken in the belief of them. Review, again and again, the evidences of the miraculous incarnation of Jesus. Behold the spirit of prophecy, declaring, ages before it came to pass, the conception of the Virgin, and the birth of the Messiah. See the event exactly fulfilled at the time predicted, in the person of our Lord: and when you have fully impressed your mind with the proper conviction due to these undeniable testimonies, then go on, and attend to that wonderful train of conduct which followed in the life of Christ, discriminating him from every other being merely human; and then determine whether such an happy concurrence of circumstances does not clearly ascertain the real dignity and character of our blessed Master. You cannot but conclude with the prophet, that he was "Emmanuel, God with us;" or as the apostle emphatically called him, "God manifest in the flesh," (1 Tim. iii. 16.)

Convinced, then, that the birth of Jesus was miraculous, we no longer wonder when we hear him asserting his relationship with the Father, and behold events in his life every way demonstrable of the GODHEAD of his person. Nor from being equally assured, at the same time, that he was of the "seed of the woman," (Gal. iv. 4,) are we astonished to find actions suitable to such an offspring. This union of our nature in the person of our Lord, serves to explain what otherwise would be unaccountable, and even contradictory. The prophets which described the Messiah under the greatest and most lofty distinctions, foretold also that "he should grow up as a tender plant, and as a root out of a dry ground; that he had no form or comeliness, and when we should see him there was no beauty that we should desire him," (Isa. liii. 2.) Hence, therefore, when we read in the history of Jesus, that "the child grew, and waxed strong in spirit: that he increased in wisdom and in stature, (Luke ii. 52.); that he was subject to all the wants and infirmities of our nature; of *hunger*, and *thirst*, and *cold*, and *weariness;* was *afflicted* and *troubled in spirit;* was open to impressions of joy and sorrow: in short, that he was a man, and felt as a man upon all occasions; let not these things stagger your faith in the GODHEAD of Jesus. Recollect that these are the very circumstances the prophets taught us to expect. The proofs of our Lord's humanity, when connected with the testimony of his divinity also, are no less proofs of his being the Messiah. This union of two natures is the very criterion of his character. Had Christ wanted this evidence, though coming in all the power of the Highest, and bringing with him every other credential of his being the Son of God, yet would he not have answered the description the prophets had given of the Messiah, unless, at the same time, he came as the Son of man.

The want of attending to those discriminating characters by which the Messiah was to be known, is the great, and perhaps the only cause of all that unhappy dissension in the church of Christ, concerning the real dignity of our blessed Redeemer. Alas! that ever Christians should have read the Scriptures with so little discernment, after Jesus "hath sent his angel to testify unto the churches, that he is both the root and the offspring of David," (Rev. xxii. 16.) As the *root*, his pre-existence proves his GODHEAD, and as the *offspring*, it effectually shews his humanity: and both together form the united qualities which were to constitute the Messiah. Whatever we meet with in the expressions of Christ or his apostles, when speaking of our Lord as a man, so far from lessening the Redeemer's character in our esteem, ought to confirm our faith the more; for it clearly and unequivocally proves him to be the Messiah, of whom these things are said. Did the sacred writers indeed represent him as a man *only*, and no more, the case would be different. He would then be deficient in one part of the character predicted, and consequently could not be the Messiah. But we have already seen how amply the servants of our Lord have borne testimony to his GODHEAD;* and we as readily, and as cheerfully receive their testimony also to the proofs they give of his humanity; for it is from both we derive our assurance that Jesus is the Christ.

How mysterious soever this unity may appear in one and the same person, it is evident that the great end of our Redeemer's mission could not have been accomplished without it. And the question why so awful a dispensation became necessary for the purpose of our redemption as the incarnation of the Son of God, will only give rise to others of the like nature, which are easier asked than explained. In short, in this, as well as many other cases, we perceive that "God's thoughts are not our thoughts, nor his ways our ways," (Isa. lv. 8.) The "preaching of the cross," and "Christ crucified, was to the Jews of old a stumbling-block, and to the Greeks foolishness;" and so it will ever appear to the wisdom of this world; but as an apostle assures us, to "them which are called, both Jews and Greeks, it is Christ the power of God, and the wisdom of God."†

---

* See the Second Sermon.

† 1 Cor. i. 23, 24. The mysterious union of natures in the person of Jesus, besides the great object intended by it, that he might become "a sacrifice for sin;" was designed to answer another important purpose, namely, that he might be a *Mediator* at the right hand of power. The consideration of the Redeemer under this exalted character, is in my apprehension, so decisive an evidence, to the GODHEAD of his person, that I could wish it had been attended to in a more awakened manner, than I believe it hath been generally regarded. For my own part, I cannot possibly conceive, how Jesus can be thought competent to the character of a Mediator, unless he be supposed to possess those properties resulting from the union of the divine nature with the human, which can alone qualify to the performance of it. As this view of the subject is to me particularly striking, I hope the reader will indulge the desire of adding an observation upon it, and will give it also his particular attention.

The apostle Paul in his Epistle to Timothy hath observed, that "there is one God and one Mediator between God and men, the man Christ Jesus." And from hence the unbeliever in Christ's GODHEAD hath been led to suppose, that he hath discovered in this text somewhat to satisfy his mind, in his system of infidelity. But this idea altogether arises, from a misapprehension of the motive for which the apostle at

The events which followed in the life of Jesus, correspond with his miraculous incarnation. The myste-

that time was so particular, in dwelling only on the *manhood* of Jesus. It should be remembered, that he was then speaking of the Redeemer in his *Mediatorial* character. And in that character, it was absolutely necessary, to mention expressly the human nature of Christ. It certainly was a point of much consequence, to recollect that the human, as well as the divine nature of Jesus, was employed in that endearing character. The apostle knew how apt the mind, in the contemplation of what is great, is prompted to overlook what is important; and while beholding the exalted Saviour at the right-hand of power, might forget the manhood in the GODHEAD. And as the recollection of Jesus in both natures became a matter inconceivably interesting to the soul, more particularly at those sacred seasons when approaching the throne of grace; the apostle hereby rendered the whole representation most gracious and accommodating, in reminding the faithful, that *that* Mediator, through whom alone they could draw nigh, was " the man Christ Jesus." As if he had said, ' When at any time from a deep sense of sin, and a conscious state of unworthiness, you feel the soul depressed, and kept back, from drawing nigh the mercy-seat; let the recollection of the Redeemer's personal experience of human infirmities give you encouragement.' ' He was in all points like as we are, sin only excepted.' But before any one presumes from hence to conclude that the apostle, by this express mention of the human nature of Jesus, meant to intimate, that he considered the man Christ Jesus as a man *only;* I would beg to refer him to a passage, in the same apostle's writings to the Galatians; and desire him to explain, upon the same principles, in what sense we are thus to accept the apostle's phrase, in relation to the person of Jesus. The passage I allude to is in the first chapter of that epistle: in which Paul is modestly asserting the authority of his commission, from the consideration of the manner in which he obtained it, and the dignity of him from whom it came. " I neither received it (says he) of man, neither was I taught it, but by the revelation of Jesus Christ." Here the subject is reversed. The human nature of Jesus is not noticed. Nay, if abstractedly considered, and without reference to any other part of the scripture by way of explanation, it is denied: for Paul says, he did not receive his commission from *man,* and yet he had it from Jesus Christ. But surely no one would suppose that the apostle meant it should be understood, that he denied the humanity of Jesus? From this comparative view of those texts of scripture, the reason seems sufficiently plain why in the one the apostle dwells so expressly on the *manhood,* and in the other intimates only the *Godhead* of Jesus: because it more immediately corresponded with his subject, and was directed to answer that point of doctrine which he had then in view before him.

But though I venture to think that this statement is very clear, and liable to no exception; yet I beg it may be understood, that it is not from hence only that I draw my conclusion. It is principally from the consideration of the character of a Mediator as it is in itself, and more

rious volume opens with "God manifest in the flesh," (1 Tim. iii. 16,) and every page in the sacred history car-

---

especially when that character is performed by the Son of God, that I feel conviction of the GODHEAD of his person. And so perfectly clear and decided a point I confess it is to me, that I only wonder how any man can make it an article in his creed, to subscribe to the doctrine of Jesus as a Mediator, and yet suppose him not to possess one part of ability in the character, which is indispensable to the other.

The idea of *mediation*, is to reconcile parties who are in a state of variance. And the character of a *Mediator* is to accomplish this purpose. Hence therefore the very nature of the thing itself, presupposes in the person undertaking it, that he hath a perfect apprehension of the cause of dispute; a knowledge of the hearts and disposition of both parties; and that he possesses full powers and ability of compromising the difference. He must be what Job calls, "a days-man to lay his hand upon both," Job ix. 33. Even among men, amidst the little jarrings and animosities which spring up in life, no one is ever chosen as an umpire, to settle the point of contest by an arbitration, but who is supposed to be competent to the task, by the possession of these qualities. Apply then this reasoning to the case before us, and it must, I think, instantly strike every candid mind with full conviction, that in that awful breach which sin hath made in the enmity of our hearts to God, Jesus could not be a suitable mediator to bring about a reconciliation, unless he possessed the ability to enter into a perfect knowledge of the mind of both; and consequently therefore he must partake of the nature of both. Upon any other principles I confess I have no conception how the service can be effected. How is it possible for Jesus to be the prevailing Mediator, which he is declared to be in the scripture, if he has not the qualities of mediation? Can he know the mind of both parties, unless by a participation of the nature of both? Could he lay his hand (as Job expresses it) upon God, unless he is on an equality with God? Could he make up the quarrel between Beings so infinitely removed from each other as God and man, by proposing what might suit the honour of the former to accept, and what as man's representative the latter had to offer, unless he was perfectly acquainted with the mind of both? And could this be attained by any means short of what I am labouring to prove, that Christ partook of both natures? Let these points be but coolly and seriously considered, and I venture to persuade myself they will appear unanswerable and conclusive. I confess indeed the assumption of the manhood by the Redeemer, does not seem to have been so needful in order to qualify him to the character as Mediator; for the knowledge of our nature could not have been rendered more perfect by it, to the infinite mind of God. But this is not so immediate to my present argument. What I am chiefly, if not altogether contending for, is the expediency of the Godhead in union with the manhood, to render the person of Jesus competent to the character of a Mediator; and that Christ really possessed both. And so important I consider this point to be, so clearly proved, and so unanswerably certain, that I must

ries with it some evidence of the same mysterious subject. Did it come within the limits or design of my present plan, it would be easy to bring forward a great variety of circumstances of this kind, which occur in the evangelists. But this would necessarily lead me to be too diffuse, and particular. I must, therefore, adopt a method more comprehensive. And as I persuade myself I am now addressing a body of Christians, who are no strangers to our Lord's history, it will be sufficient to select such passages only in the life of Christ, as may be demonstrative of the great point in question.

It will answer every purpose, therefore, to shew, that there are certain particulars in the person of Christ, which set him at an infinite distance from the highest and most exalted characters among the sons of men,

---

beg, again and again, to insist upon it, and with a warmth of expression proportioned to its infinite consequence; that unless Christ did actually unite in his sacred person the *divine* with the *human* nature, I cannot see in what sense he can be considered as a Mediator, or what value such a mediation can be to his people.

Whether these observations shall appear equally satisfactory to the reader, so as to silence every doubt, and remove every scruple, must be left to his determination, with whom ultimately all conviction rests. I sincerely pray God they may afford that comfort to the eye that now reads, which they have long given to him, whose frail hand now writes; and then he will find what a peculiarly refreshing and encouraging doctrine it is in a dark and trying hour. When the soul is smitten with a sense of guilt, and the conscious corruption of the heart, and the powerful suggestions of the great enemy of darkness, pour in all their united force to restrain from prayer; what a delightful consideration is it in such seasons to look up to the throne of grace, and contemplate in our great Mediator, one "who is touched with the feelings of our infirmities," and who at the same time hath power as a Prince with God to prevail! Think of it, my brother, I entreat you, upon every occasion, when drawing nigh the throne of grace, through that channel by which alone you can approach the throne through the mediation of Jesus; and in the recollection, may the Lord strengthen your hands and heart! That almighty Friend we have now in heaven, in whose hands all our high interests are placed, though once "a man of sorrows," was, and is, no less, at the same time, "one with the Father, over all God blessed for ever." And while you contemplate in his sacred person your own nature already in glory, never forget the purpose also for which he is gone before; that it is according to his own most blessed promise, "only to prepare a place for all his people, that where he is they may be also."

whether prophets, or teachers, which have ever appeared in the world. That from the first moment of his entrance on his public character, when a voice from heaven proclaimed the dignity of his person, to the last hour of his beneficial ministry; the miracles he performed; the language he assumed; the attributes he possessed; the titles by which he is every where distinguished in Scripture; that great and awful sacrifice of his death, which he himself declared to be the immediate purpose of his mission; the concluding scenes of his life; the solemn and magnificent events which followed his death; his glorious resurrection and ascension; the fulfilment of the promise he made to his followers before his departure, of sending down the gifts of the Holy Spirit upon their hearts, and which he faithfully did; the assurance of his return again at the last day to judgment; and the expectation he taught mankind to entertain of a future and invisible world: such views of Christ (and they are but the mere outlines of a portrait which the evangelists have drawn, under divine assistance, of the Son of God) impress the mind with an awful idea of the greatness and sanctity of his character whom they represent, and justly render him the object of gratitude, adoration, and praise, to all generations of the Christian church.

To enter into a minute description of these particulars would require a separate discourse, or rather a series of discourses: either of which is inadmissible in the present work. I shall only beg your attention to such of the more prominent features of them, which appear in the life of Jesus, as may the best enable us to ascertain his real character. And among the evidences of this kind which I conceive necessary to bring forward in proof of his GODHEAD, the first place is due to that large and extensive chain of miracles which he performed; because our blessed Lord himself, upon all occasions, particularly referred to them, as carrying with them the fullest proof of a divine power in the unity he possessed with the Father.

Miracles, in confirmation of a doctrine, and as a sanction to the truth of what they are intended to testify, are not peculiar to the ministry of Jesus. Under the Old Testament, many servants of the Lord brought the same credentials with them. Moses, Joshua, Samuel, Elijah, and others, are instances of this kind: they frequently appealed to the wonderful works they wrought, as proofs that what they said and did was by divine appointment. Hence, therefore, the miracles which our Lord performed, considered abstractedly, though surpassing both in greatness and in number whatever had preceded them, do not prove his divinity: but it is the *manner*, the *declarations* which accompanied them, and the *personal authority* by which they were performed; these are the circumstances which so eminently separate the works of Jesus from any former prophet, and draw a most striking distinction between them. Such, indeed, as might reasonably be supposed to form a line of discrimination between the actions of the Lord and those of his servants. They wrought wonders to display the glory of God; "Jesus (it is said) to manifest his own."*

Let us examine, in one or two particulars, the Scripture account of miracles, under this idea, for proof of what I am asserting.

The prophets and servants of the Lord invariably declared by whose authority, and in whose name they acted; and generally addressed God in a short and expressive prayer, suitable to the moment, when about to perform some supernatural operation. This is visible, more or less, through the whole Jewish history.† But with Christ matters were very differently conducted. It appears, that in all his mighty works, he was influenced by his own immediate will and authority. "Lord, (says

* "This beginning of miracles did Jesus in Cana of Galilee, and manifested forth his glory," (says St. John,) John ii. 11.

† See Exod. viii. 12, and ix. 29—33. Joshua x. 12. 1 Sam. xii. 18. 1 Kings xvii. 20, 21.

a leper to him) if thou wilt, thou canst make me clean. I will; (says Jesus) be thou clean," (Matt. viii. 2.) Here was no previous application to heaven, but the disposition in our Lord was immediate, and the deed instantly followed. Of the same kind is the miracle of Christ raising the widow of Nain's son. It is said, that "when the Lord saw her, he had compassion on her, and said unto her, Weep not. And he came and touched the bier, and they that bare him stood still. And he said, Young man, I say unto thee, arise. And he that was dead sat up, and began to speak." All this was done without any intimation that he wrought this by any other authority than his own, (Luke vii.)

And among those who had faith to be healed of their diseases, (which Christ was pleased sometimes to make the condition on which they should receive the benefit of his mercy) it should seem they entertained the belief that Christ possessed this ability inherent in *himself*. Hence the poor woman in the throng said, "If I may but touch the hem of his garment, I shall be whole," (Mark v. 28.) And to the same purport the Centurion, "Speak the word only (says he to Christ,) and my servant shall be healed," (Matt. viii. 8.) In these and numberless instances of the same kind,* we hear not a word of Jesus acting by the power of his Father *only;* but from his own personal authority in conjunction with it.

In the case of the resurrection of Lazarus from the grave, our blessed Lord, indeed, used a short prayer, addressed to his Father, before he called him from the dead. But wherefore? Christ gave an immediate reason for it: "Because (says he) of the people which stand by, I said it, that they may believe that thou hast sent me," (John xi. 42); that is, by this evident communication, in the very moment of performing so illustrious an act as the raising of the dead, they might

* Such as the cleansing the ten lepers; the casting out devils, &c. &c.

believe, what Christ had before asserted, that all he did was in perfect unity with God; that what things soever the Father doeth, "these also doeth the Son likewise. The Father is in me (says Christ), and I in him; I and my Father are one." In the resurrection of Lazarus there is something so truly unequalled in our Lord's *manner*, both before he wrought the miracle, and at the time of performing it, that it hardly needs a reference to any other event in his history for the proof of his GODHEAD.

The solemn and authoritative discourse in which he proclaimed himself to be "the resurrection and the life;" and the miracle which immediately followed, an evidence, as it were, of the truth of his declaration; what *criteria* less than divinity could these be? We read in Scripture that prophets and messengers from God have occasionally been invested with ability to work events, truly miraculous, as the test of their commission. But what servant of Jehovah ever said of himself, "I am the resurrection and the life; he that believeth in me, though he were dead, yet shall he live; and whosoever liveth, and believeth in me, shall never die. I give unto my sheep eternal life, and they shall never perish, neither shall any man pluck them out of my hand?"* Can it be possible

* John x. 28. It hath been a stumbling-block to *infidels* and all *natural* unrenewed men, the different expressions used upon different occasions by our blessed LORD; as if there were a contradiction in them. Thus, as in this passage, "giving his sheep eternal life;" declaring himself to be "One with the Father," and the like; and yet elsewhere saying, "My Father is greater than I," (John xiv. 28.) But to a *spiritual* mind taught of God, there is nothing difficult of apprehension. In the unity and essence of the GODHEAD, there can be neither superiority, nor inferiority in one to another; for the GODHEAD is all One and the same; and in the distinction of Persons, each, and all, possess alike, all divine attributes and perfections. By keeping in remembrance, therefore, that in the Holy Trinity all are equal; it will follow, that whatever is spoken of one, which is not of another, of those divine Persons, that carries an idea with it of inferiority, can only refer to the distinct and separate acts wrought by each in the "covenant of grace." One of the sacred Persons in the GODHEAD graciously taking into union with himself that holy portion of our nature, and thereby becoming the surety of his church

for *eternal life* to be the gift of any but an *eternal Being?* There is something surely in these expressions, totally

---

and people, became no less the servant of JEHOVAH in his Trinity of Persons, to fulfil the law for us; while the indwelling GODHEAD still preserved a perfect equality with the Father and the HOLY GHOST. And here is the key to open and explain every difficulty of this kind to be met with in the gospel.

I have often lamented to hear gracious souls at a loss to unriddle difficulties as they appear to their view; which are no riddles at all. And I have myself in times past, spent days, yea, weeks, to reconcile passages of Scripture, supposed to be foreign to each other, which never were at variance. Our LORD's explanation of that problem, John iii. 13, solves every other; and if I might venture to say as much, without offence, I would add, that the sole cause wherefore children taught of God, are ever entangled with difficulties of this kind is, when they lose sight of the Holy Trinity. For, if instead of having this always at the *bottom* of the whole transactions of the "covenant of grace," we take parts and portions of the "covenant of grace," and explain them according to our standard and reasoning of things, it cannot fail but different shades will be formed by such reasoning. For every *effect,* both in time and in eternity, there must have been a *cause.* The covenant of grace is the *effect* of that *cause,* which hath the pleasure, counsel, will of JEHOVAH, in his Trinity of Persons, for its origin before all worlds; in which each glorious Person took an equal part; and the whole three Persons, constituting One and the same undivided JEHOVAH, have come forward to the church in all those endeared and endearing acts of love, which shew the perfect love of each, and their equality in the possession of all divine attributes.

It is on this account, and with a view ever to keep in remembrance those divine standards of character in the HOLY THREE, which bear record in heaven, I never allow myself to speak of the sacred Persons which constitute One and the same GODHEAD, as *first,* or *second,* or *third.* I know that many of my brethren, both in the ministry and out of it, do so, and I presume not to impugn their judgment; for myself, I never do it. The very priority of term, I know not how it is, but so it is, naturally connects with the expression a precedency, or superiority; and as the HOLY GHOST hath furnished sacred names to these sacred Persons in his sacred Scriptures, I always confine myself to them. That declaration, 1 John v. 7, is beautiful, "For there are Three that bear record in heaven: the FATHER, the WORD, and the HOLY GHOST; and these Three are ONE." Whether I am correct in this I do not determine; but I certainly follow Scripture. For there is not a verse in the Bible which authorizes the LORD's people to call one *first,* or another *second.* The spiritual reader will do well to sit at the feet of Jesus at all times, and upon all occasions, for his divine teaching. In this twilight of being, the highest taught child of GOD seeth divine things only as through a glass darkly. Ere long we shall come to open day-light, "when we shall see Him as He is, and know, even as we are known."

different from the words of any former prophet, and extremely difficult to be accounted for, on the presumption that Jesus, upon all these occasions, though speaking personally, meant nothing more than a derived power from his Father. Would Christ (supposing him to be no more than man) have distinguished himself by such eternal attributes, and spoken so confidently of his own power, without continually qualifying the expression with a proper caution in what sense it was to be understood; that the whole was derivative, and that he himself was no more than the instrument of his Father? When we behold Christ, therefore, in this striking instance now under consideration, taking a title unknown before, calling himself "the resurrection and the life;" and immediately, in proof of it, bringing back a dead man from the grave, stopping the very principles of corruption in a lifeless mass, and causing him to re-assume animation: I cannot conceive such a manifestation of divine power to imply less than a divine agent; and as we justly infer omnipotence from the works of creation, so we may equally, in this instance, conclude it could only be the exertion of the same power in a resurrection: and both, we find, were wrought by the Son of God.

Compare now the actions of the most favoured servants of God, with the wonderful miracles of our divine Lord, and see whether, in a single instance, any of them were distinguished in this manner. Did ever any prophet assume a language like that of Jesus, or give the least reason to suppose, as Christ hath done, that it was by virtue of an intimate union with the Father his mighty works were all accomplished? Nay, do they not all of them expressly declare, that every thing they said or wrought was in the name of the Lord? This circumstance, I conceive to be particularly striking, and proper to be well attended to in our comparison of the miracles of Christ with those of the prophets; for it forms a manifest distinction between them, and such (as I before observed), as may justly be supposed to discriminate the words and actions of the Lord from those of his servants.

But, besides this discrimination in the *manner* by which our Lord wrought his miracles, some of them were of that *nature* also, that they carry with them no possible resemblance to those of his servants.

When we read that "Jesus went about doing good, healing all manner of sickness, and all manner of disease among the people, (Matt. iv. 23;) that wheresoever he entered, into villages, or cities, or the country, they laid the sick in the streets, and besought him that they might touch, if it were but the border of his garment; and as many as touched him were made perfectly whole," (Mark vi. 56.) Wonderful as this description is, it gives but an imperfect idea of the greatness of Christ's character. But to have seen him casting out devils, bringing demoniacs instantly from a state of phrensy to perfect calmness and composure, the dead resuming life at his command, and the waves of the sea becoming still at his voice. Oh! could an infidel have been present at scenes of this nature, which the Son of God daily performed, or could any of those who allow the religion of Jesus to be a revelation from heaven, but yet deny the GODHEAD of him who gave it to us: could they, I say, but have beheld our glorious GOD thus continually exercising his power and authority, what irresistible conviction would have taken place in every mind!* How

* I have stated the above very strongly, on the supposition that men were open to conviction, and not steeled with prejudices, in a predetermination not to acknowledge the truth. Hence we read, that while *some*, at the resurrection of *Lazarus*, were overpowered with the contemplation of the mighty deed of CHRIST in raising him from the dead; *others*, who equally saw it, went their way to inform the Pharisees of it, and sought "the more to destroy Jesus?" John xi. 45, 46. But added to the predilection of the human mind by the fall, to disbelieve the record GOD hath given of his Son; there is another, and if possible a more powerful one, namely, the want of spiritual faculties, to apprehend the spiritual truths of GOD. I state this the rather, that if the reader be

admirably were the words of the Psalmist verified upon many of those occasions! "The waters saw thee, O God; the waters saw thee, and were afraid, the depths also were troubled," (Psalm lxxvii. 16.) "He ruleth both the raging of the sea, and the noise of his waves, and the madness of the people," (Psalm lxv. 7.)

But chiefly, what raises Christ above all parallel, are the wonderful events which attended the concluding scenes of our Lord's ministry; for these are evidently to be classed among the miracles of Jesus. What unspeakable dignity must have appeared in the person of our Lord, when his presence struck to the ground the band of men and officers which came to apprehend him! What awful circumstances of a superior nature did his agony in the garden intimate! Above all, what unheard-of events were those which attended his death, when they wrought such an instantaneous conviction upon the most obdurate breasts! The prodigies which solemnized his last moments, darkness covering the whole land, the rending of the vail of the temple, the quaking of the earth, the opening of graves, even the bodies of men arising from their tombs, and appearing unto many; such convulsions of nature surely imply a superior dignity in his person, whose death they witnessed: and when viewed in connection with the magnificent scenes which followed his glorious resurrection and ascension, and the sending down the gifts of the Holy Ghost; these astonishing events altogether exalt our Lord above all comparison, and leave at an infinite distance, every

---

spiritually taught, he may thankfully look at the source from whence that divine life originates, and bless God for distinguishing mercy. And he ought to know from that divine teaching, why it is, and how it is, he differs from another. Until we are regenerated from the *Adam* fall transgression, we have no spiritual faculties to apprehend divine things. What our glorious LORD said to the miserable man in torments, holds universally true in every other instance. The unawakened in trespasses and sins would not, yea, could not, "be persuaded though one rose from the dead," (Luke xvi. 31.)

worker of miracles, when mentioned with the Son of God.

And still further, as a discriminating mark in the miracles of Jesus, we find they were sometimes accompanied with the exertion of another proof of divine authority, namely, *the forgiveness of sins.* A power which our Lord's most inveterate enemies acknowledge could only be the prerogative of God; but which Christ assumed, and exercised repeatedly.

He pardoned *the Sinner* which washed his feet in the house of Simon the Pharisee, (Luke vii. 34, *et seq.*) He forgave *the Woman* who was taken in adultery, (John viii.) He cancelled the sins of the *penitent Thief* on the cross, in the moment of departure, and assured him of happiness, (Luke xxiii.) And the sins of the *Paralytic*, who was brought to him to be healed of his infirmity, he declared to be forgiven; and immediately wrought the cure on his body, as a confirmation of the mercy he had granted to his soul, (Mark ii.) Are these the deeds of a mere man? Was it ever known or ever heard that any prophet, any servant, or messenger from God, spake or acted in this manner? Would the meek and unassuming temper of Jesus have done this? Nay, would God himself have given a sanction to such usurpation? Surely that great and jealous Lord, who hath left upon everlasting record the most awful examples of his anger at the least encroachment upon his name or authority, would have checked the daring attempt, if Jesus had been no more than man, and thus made himself equal with God. He who caused the earth to open her mouth, and swallow up "Korah and his company," for presuming only to enter upon the priestly office, (Numb. xvi.) who made the hand of *Jeroboam* to wither for speaking rashly, (1 Kings xiii.) and struck *Uzzah* instantly dead for touching the ark, (2 Sam. vi.) would never have suffered such repeated instances of blasphemy to have escaped unpunished, much less have justified, and given the most decided approbation to the whole, by honouring our Lord's cause with the continual operation of miracles. Nothing can more fully demonstrate the GODHEAD of our divine LORD: and the proof which Christ proposed to try it by, in the evidence of the cure he wrought on the cripple, was the clearest and most incontestable that could be desired. When, therefore, you find that the paralytic instantly arose at the command of Jesus, took up the bed whereon he lay, and went forth glorifying God, you will not hesitate to cry out with the centurion, who received his conviction at the foot of the cross, "Doubtless this is the Son of God."

But, lastly, the highest and finishing distinction of all, between Christ, and every other instructor of mankind, who performed miracles in confirmation of his commission, is the power which Jesus possessed and actually employed, of conferring on his disciples the ability of producing effects similar to those which he himself had wrought, as so many proofs that they derived their authority from him.

Even in the life-time of Christ, and before the Holy Ghost was imparted, this power was given to them. They were sent "to preach the gospel, and to heal the sick; to cleanse the lepers, to raise the dead, and cast out devils," (Matt. x. 8.) And when they returned with an account of the success of their embassy, they ascribed the whole to his personal name and authority. "Even the devils (they said) are subject to us through thy name." Upon which our blessed Lord made use of these remarkable expressions; "I beheld Satan as lightning fall from heaven: Behold, I give unto you power to tread on serpents, and scorpions, and over all the power of the enemy, and nothing shall by any means hurt you," (Luke x. 17—19.) And after our Lord's ascension, and the descent of the divine Spirit, the commission was enlarged to a still further extent of power, according to the promise of Jesus, that "not only the works which he himself had done should they do, but greater works than these," (John xiv. 12.) But the same authority of the master was still preserved. "In my name shall they cast out devils; they shall speak with new tongues; they shall take up serpents, and if they drink any deadly thing it shall not hurt them; they shall lay hands on the sick, and they shall recover," (Mark xvi. 18.) Thus the whole was to be accomplished in the name, and by the power of Christ. Hence we find, upon every occasion, the apostles working signs and wonders under this authority, which they had received from their Master. "In the name of Jesus Christ of Nazareth, rise up and walk," said Peter to the cripple, at the gate of the temple, (Acts iii. 6.) "Eneas (saith the same apostle), Jesus Christ maketh thee whole," (Acts ix. 34.) "Brother Saul (said Ananias), the Lord, even Jesus that appeared unto thee in the way as thou camest, hath sent me that thou mightest receive thy sight, and be filled with the Holy Ghost," (Acts ix. 17.) "I command thee, in the name of Jesus Christ of Nazareth to come out of her," said Paul to the damsel possessed with a spirit of divination, (Acts xvi. 18.) From all which instances it is evident the apostles considered the ability they possessed, to be derived immediately from him in whose name, and by whose authority they acted. And "his name, through faith in his name," (Acts iii. 16,) was the universal charm by which all their miracles were wrought.

Indeed, Peter, for himself and his brethren, solemnly declared, that the wonderful deeds which were performed by them were wholly to be ascribed to the power of Christ. "Why look ye (says he to the people, who were struck with admiration at the cure of the cripple in Solomon's porch), why look ye so earnestly on us, as though by our own power or holiness we had made this man to walk?" (Acts iii. 12.) "Be it known unto you all, and to all the people of Israel, that by the name of Jesus Christ of Nazareth, whom ye crucified, whom

God raised from the dead, even by him, doth this man stand here before you whole," (Acts iv. 10.)

Now, then, review the whole of the argument in favour of our Lord's GODHEAD, as it arises from the miracles of Christ, and those of his apostles wrought in his name. Examine with the most rigid strictness the many instances of a supernatural power with which Jesus performed his mighty works, totally different from every servant of God, both in the *manner* by which they were accomplished, and in the *nature* of the miracles themselves. Consider also the additional testimony in the ability Jesus imparted to his disciples of doing the same wonderful deeds as he himself had wrought. And to the whole subjoin the peculiar evidence of the supreme power and authority Christ exercised in the forgiveness of sins, with which his miracles were not unfrequently accompanied, and which is, without all doubt, the highest and most finished proof of divinity; and then question whether it be possible to believe that any being, merely human, could possess such properties! Surely, if we would but view things coolly and dispassionately, there arises from hence such a strength of testimony, to prove the divinity of Jesus, as ought to carry conviction to every candid mind.

But the miracles of Jesus, and those wrought in his name by his servants the apostles, though they afford such incontestable evidences of his divinity, yet are they by no means the only proofs we meet with in the life of Christ of this important doctrine. The blessed Redeemer manifested others equally great and convincing. The *language* he assumed, and the *authoritative manner* in which he discoursed with his disciples upon many occasions; these are another species of testimony which clearly prove his nature to have been more than human. And when we discover also in his life, that he possessed *divine attributes*, and is distinguished by the sacred writings under *divine titles*, which are the well-known incommunicable distinctions of the GODHEAD: when we behold these properties all uniting in the formation of his character, they cannot leave the mind in a moment's suspense whether he be not God, " in whom (as the apostle expresses it) are hid all the treasures of wisdom and knowledge," (Colos. ii. 3.)

But the consideration of these, and other particulars yet remaining to be noticed in our Lord's character, would necessarily lead me beyond the usual limits. And it would be proper at present to relieve your attention. I desire, therefore, to leave you to the full impression of what hath been already said, with an humble supplication to the throne of grace, that the light of God's Holy Spirit may precede our steps in the paths of truth, and lead us to the full discovery of that knowledge which may make us wise unto salvation, through Jesus Christ our Lord.

SERMON VI.

JOHN VII. 46.

Never man spake like this Man.

In tracing the accomplishment of prophecy concerning the Messiah, in the person of our most glorious Christ, the preceding discourse was principally intended to point out proofs of our blessed Lord's possessing that mysterious unity of nature which was predicted should constitute the Messiah's character. The evidences brought before you to substantiate the claim of Jesus to this distinguishing peculiarity, in demonstrating that his birth was altogether miraculous, were, I hope, convincing and unanswerable. And the subsequent events in our Lord's history (as far as we have yet proceeded in the subject) tended no less to prove that his nature was more than human. The testimony derived from the peculiar *manner* and *authority* by which Christ wrought his miracles, and imparted ability to his disciples in *his name* to perform theirs, carries with it (as I then observed to you) a species of evidence in support of his GODHEAD, which, I am sure, will appear more satisfactory the more it is attended to.

It was impossible in that discourse to comprise the whole of the arguments to this doctrine as they arise from the incidents in the life of Christ. I have now, therefore, reassumed the topic, in order to finish what was then unavoidably postponed; and to examine, with the same fairness and impartiality, the other testimonies on this subject which appear in our Lord's character.

The first to which I shall beg your attention is, that which is suggested in the words of the text; I mean the *unparalleled discourses* of Christ: for these certainly very highly express a peculiar dignity in his person.

Among the ancient prophets we can clearly discern the credentials of the commission by which they acted. The system of morality delivered by Moses was evidently a divine system; and, as far as it extended, differed in nothing from that of Jesus Christ. But it is not in the moral part of the gospel only we are to look for traces of our Lord's greatness of character, but in the whole scope and tendency of his religion taken altogether. The preceptive doctrines of Christianity are perhaps the least from whence we derive evidences of the divinity of its blessed Author. Much higher proofs abound from the peculiar and distinguishing points of his religion. His solemn assurances that the great purport of his embassy was to expiate the sins of our nature; the language he assumed when expressing this awful truth; the personal authority by which he proclaimed pardon to the penitent and faithful in this world, and happiness in that which is to come: the divine wisdom by which he uttered these, and the like doctrines, and the divine power by which he declared he would accomplish the whole of his designs, by "drawing all men unto him," (John xii. 32,) these are among the unequalled subjects of our Lord's discourses, which fully prove that "he spake as never man spake."

It will not be required of me that I should select from the gospel any particular passages to establish the truth of this observation. The fact itself will more fully appear by a reference to the New Testament. Let me beg of you to examine the words of Jesus by the severest test of criticism, and see whether it be possible to account, either for the *sum* and *substance* of what he taught, or the *manner* in which he delivered his doctrines to the world, upon any other supposition than of his being more than man. I conceive the strongest evidence will result from this review of our Lord's discourses in favour of his GODHEAD, and it is such as will admit of the greatest stress being laid upon it.

All the former teachers of mankind in the will of God, delivered their message with a solemn declaration in whose name they came, "Thus saith the Lord:" but Jesus gives his precepts in a tone of personal authority. "Behold, I say unto you," is the usual form with which Christ prefaced his commandments. And his invitation to his people to embrace his gracious terms of salvation runs in the same style, as from himself. "Come unto me, (is the language made use of when calling them to his gospel) all ye that travail and are heavy laden, and I will give you rest," (Matt. xi. 28.) "If any one come unto me, I will in no wise cast him out," (John vi. 37.) Who among the prophets ever opened their commission in terms like these? Well might the people be astonished (as it is said they were) at his doctrine, for this was teaching, no doubt, "as one that had authority, and not as the Scribes," (Matt. vii. 29.)

But though this manner of speaking is so peculiar to our Lord, and very strongly marks the dignity of his person, yet these are but the slightest and most inconsiderable instances of the wisdom and spirit by which he spake. When Christ dwells upon the great and interesting doctrines of his gospel, his language rises to a much higher degree of sublimity. "And all bare him witness (the evangelist informs us) and wondered at the gracious words which proceeded out of his mouth," (Luke iv. 22.) What numberless proofs of this unequalled dignity do we find in every page of the gospel! "In this place is one greater than the temple," (Matt. xii. 6.) "The Son of man is Lord even of the Sabbath day," (Matt. viii. 1.) "I am the living bread which came down from heaven. If any man eat of this bread, he shall live for ever; and the bread which I shall give is my flesh, which I will give for the life of the world," (John vi. 51.) "If any man thirst, let him come unto me and drink. He that believeth on me (as the Scripture saith) out of his belly shall flow rivers of living water," (John vii. 37, 38.) When we trace through the whole tenor of our Lord's discourses a vein of language like this, and attested by a train of events equally great and mysterious; when we hear him also, declaring himself to be the *resurrection* and the *life*, and that he possesses the supreme power of *raising the dead*, and finally determining the fate of all the race of men; that "the hour is coming when all that are in their graves shall hear his voice, and come forth," (John v. 28); and that the rewards of fidelity, and the punishments to disobedience, will wholly result from *his* determination: surely there is something in all this, which defines the character of the Son of God most perfectly, and draws an everlasting line of separation, between the person of Jesus and the highest of the sons of men. In short, let us only suppose the Divine Being was to descend from heaven, and to live and converse with mankind, as Christ did; what greater evidence could we desire, in proof of the greatness of his nature, than our Lord gave in the spirit and wisdom by which he daily spake? And whoever reads the discourses of our Lord as they are found in the gospel, fairly and candidly, and with an unprejudiced mind, will be frequently induced, during the perusal, to make the same observation which the Jewish officers did in the text, "Never man spake like this man."*

* However decisive to the great point in question, the evidence arising from our Lord's unequalled manner of speaking may be, in the outward ministry of the word; there is yet a much higher proof, arising from the same cause, which I pray God the reader may possess, for without the attainment of it, indeed, the other is nothing worth: I mean, when the inward effect of the words of Jesus is applied by the Holy Ghost to the heart of man. Men may assent to the great truths of the gospel, from the mere conviction of the understanding, without being at all interested in them as so many principles of conduct: and this, it is

The next argument in proof of our blessed Lord's Deity, arising from the circumstances of his life, may be taken from the divine *attributes* which he possessed. And as these are clearly among the peculiar character of GODHEAD, the only object I shall have to accomplish, will be to prove the certainty of the thing itself, that these properties were in the person of Jesus. Some of them, indeed, are so evident, that we can plainly discover them ourselves, in the words and actions of Christ; and others are so fully ascribed to him by the apostles and inspired writers, that there can be no hesitation in concluding that he possessed them. A few quotations from scripture will be sufficient to our purpose.

Omnipresence is so peculiar an attribute of GODHEAD, that our Lord's possessing this perfection would of itself be sufficient to determine the certainty of his

---

to be apprehended, by what is daily manifested in the world, is the case of thousands; but this is perfectly a distinct thing from the operation of the voice of Jesus in the heart. "His sheep hear his voice; and he calleth his own sheep by name, and leadeth them out; they know his voice and follow him." Terms these, which evidently demonstrate, that there is somewhat more implied than the mere *outward* ministry of the word: and that an *inward* powerful effect accompanies it. They are *his sheep* which hear his voice; *them* he calls by *name;* speaking directly to their minds and consciences by a personal application; as in the case of *Paul* in the road to *Damascus*, when "they that were journeying with him saw indeed the light and were afraid, but heard not the voice of him that spake." They knew his voice by its effect. "I shall never forget thy word," (says David). And why? because, "by it thou hast quickened me." And hence the apostle Paul could tell the Thessalonians, that their election of God was known: because "our gospel" (says he) "came not unto you in word only, but also in power, and in the Holy Ghost, and in much assurance." I cannot more effectually serve the reader, than in recommending him to an earnest and diligent enquiry after the evidence of these things. However, in the general, satisfied you may be of the GODHEAD of Jesus, from this proof of the unparalleled manner in which he spake; I am most awfully convinced, that you have not yet heard him to the great and effectual purposes of salvation, unless that voice which first commanded the light to shine out of darkness "hath shined in your heart to give you the light of the knowledge of the glory of God in the face of Jesus Christ," (2 Cor. iv. 6.) Beg of God, therefore, for this unspeakable gift, and say in the language of the church, "Thou that dwellest in the gardens, the companions hearken to thy voice: cause me to hear it," (Song viii. 13.)

divine nature; for what less than an Infinite Being can fill infinite space? We shall require nothing more to substantiate the fact of our Lord's ubiquity than his own declarations. During the course of his ministry he had assured his disciples, that where "two or three are gathered together in his name, there is he in the midst of them," (Matthew xvii. 20.) "And if any man love me," (says Christ) "my Father will love him, and we will come unto him, and make our abode with him," (John xiv. 23.) And agreeably to this, in his last interview with the apostles, when he gave them his final commission to go into all the world, and preach the gospel to every creature, he confirmed this assurance of his perpetual presence: "Lo, I am with you always, even unto the end of the world," (Matthew xxviii. 20.) Such proofs of the omnipresence of the Lord, and founded on his own solemn declarations, shew in what sense it is we are authorised to infer the GODHEAD of Jesus, from his possession of this peculiar and distinguishing attribute of the Godhead.*

* The perpetual presence of the LORD with his people, besides the testimony it carries with it of his GODHEAD, opens another source of divine consolation, to the church, in the perpetual manifestations the LORD gives to them of his presence; and when known and felt and lived upon, produceth in the spiritual mind, "a joy unspeakable and full of glory, receiving the end of our faith, even the salvation of our souls." Our adorable LORD promised this, before his return to glory, when assuring his disciples, that not only He himself would come, "but the FATHER would come, and make their abode with them: and the HOLY GHOST would abide with them for ever," (John xiv. 23, 16.) All the blissful events of communion which John speaks of, (1 John i. 1—4.) arise out of this. For as every *effect* must have a *cause;* so here, the effect of our joy, arises from this cause of the presence, and manifestation, of the HOLY THREE in ONE, agreeable to *John's* statement; "if we love Him, it is because he first loved us," (1 John iv. 19.) I glanced somewhat at this subject before, in the Preface; but the several acts of the gracious manifestation of the Holy Trinity to the Church; and the calling forth of the faith and affection of the Church in return; these are not only blessed attestations of the GODHEAD of CHRIST, in confirmation of his promises; but also open to such a precious communion, between the LORD and his people, as are among the highest felicities in a life of faith, as can only be exceeded in a life

Omnipresence necessarily includes another of the incommunicable perfections, namely, *Omniscience.* The

---

of open vision in glory, that I make no apology for drawing my reader's attention to it in a short note.

It needs not be insisted upon by way of establishing the reality of the blessedness itself: that as JEHOVAH, in his Trinity of Persons, hath graciously condescended to make himself known unto his people by distinct acts of love by which each is personally revealed; so hath the LORD engaged under these distinctions of character to visit and make himself known unto them. Hence GOD our FATHER having himself chosen every one of them, and revealed himself as their FATHER in CHRIST; so he hath very blessedly said, that as this is to the adoption of children in CHRIST, they shall know him as their FATHER; and shall come to him as their FATHER; "the SPIRIT bearing witness with their spirits that they are children of God," (Jer. iii. 4, 19; Rom. viii. 14.) Hence therefore, if by regeneration, I, or you, are conscious of this relationship, and spiritually feel our souls comforted under these precious assurances of GOD the FATHER's everlasting love: is it possible to live a day without the goings forth of the *spirit* in desires after and communion with our FATHER, whose very adoption of his Church is for this express purpose here in grace, and hereafter in glory? GOD our FATHER hath not simply chosen his Church, for heaven, or happiness in another world. He hath not adopted them for kingdoms or empires: but for Himself. "This people have I formed for myself: they shall shew forth my praise," (Isaiah xliii. 21; Psalm iv. 3.) The same may be said, yea, and must be said, of each of the other glorious Persons in the GODHEAD, (Rev. iii. 20.) The whole book of the Songs, (1 Cor. vi. 19.) And let me not be thought harsh or unkind, for I mean it in the greatest affection, when I add, that among all the evidences of the renewed life, this is the nighest and the best; namely, "fellowship with the FATHER and with his SON JESUS CHRIST," (1 John i. 3.) It is very blessed, to go to ordinances and the several means of grace, when led by the HOLY GHOST: Communion with the LORD's people when the savour of his presence is known, and felt, in the assembly, is also blessed: but there may be, and the best of the Lord's people will, I believe, be ready to confess, that sometimes, and not unfrequently, there are other causes, than singly with an eye to the LORD's glory, the LORD's people attend prayer-meetings and assemblies of a like nature. But for you, or me, to retire from all society of men to enjoy communion with GOD; here can be no delusion. Hence I venture to make conclusion, not unsimilar to what the HOLY GHOST commanded John the Baptist to make in his apprehension of the person of CHRIST. "He that sent me to baptize with water, (said John) the same said unto me: Upon whom thou shalt see the SPIRIT descending, and remaining on him, the same is He which baptizeth with the HOLY GHOST. And I saw (said John) and bare record, that this is the SON of GOD," (John i. 31—34.) In humble imitation and under the same unction we may form a scriptural judgment of the true

continual presence of a Being uncircumscribed by space, and unlimited in operation, naturally implies his continual observation. And Jesus had given so many proofs of his possessing this faculty during his abode upon earth, that his disciples universally ascribed it to him upon all occasions. Our Lord perceived the woman in the throng who had touched him, (Matthew ix. 20.) He knew that *Lazarus* was dead before he proceeded to Bethany, (John xi. 14.) He knew the poor man at the pool of Bethesda, had been a long time labouring under his infirmity, (John v. 6.) He penetrated the hearts of the Scribes and Pharisees, and beheld the scheme that was forming against him, and by his words intimidated them from putting it, at that time, into execution, (Luke xx. 26.) By a look only upon Peter, he convinced him that he knew of his denial; and by a word to his disciples, he intimated that he was no stranger to their intentions. In short, it would be tedious to enumerate all the instances we meet with in the Evangelists, in proof of our Lord's omniscience. It was the exercise of this perfection which wrought conviction in the heart of Nathaniel, that Jesus was the Messiah, and drew from him in consequence of it, that ever memorable confession, that Christ was the Son of God, and King of Israel, (John i. 49.) It was the same which made the apostle Peter cry out, "Lord, thou knowest all things, thou knowest that I love thee," (John xxi. 17.) And hence we hear the frequent observation in our Lord's history, that "Jesus knew their thoughts. He knew that they were desirous to ask him," and accordingly reasoned with them upon the subject, just as if they had communicated their sentiments. "He knew all men, (says St. John) and needed not that any should testify of man, for he knew what was in

---

followers of the LORD. Where the HOLY GHOST hath descended and remaineth, and communion with the HOLY THREE in ONE is daily known and lived upon: here is the child of GOD!

man," (ii. 25.) Jesus knew in himself that his disciples murmured at him, (John vi. 61.) He knew from the beginning who they were that believed not, and who should betray him, (John xiii. 11.) Nothing can more fully prove a Divine Being possessing divine powers than such facts as these! Christ therefore gave this unequivocal testimony of himself during his abode upon earth; but the full display of this great attribute is reserved for that day when "the Lord will come to judgment, to bring to light the hidden things of darkness, and to make manifest the counsels of the heart."*

The eternity of the Son of God may, in a great measure, be inferred from what hath been already shown.† Both from his own declarations, and the character in which the sacred writers have considered him as the Creator, and Preserver of the universe, we have full authority to conclude that his goings forth were, as the prophet declared of him, from everlasting, for he

---

* 1 Cor. iv. 5. To avoid prolixity I have not noticed in the body of the discourse, (what must ever be considered a very strong additional evidence of our Lord's GODHEAD) the prescience he manifested concerning future events. Some of them were of that nature, that, to all human apprehension, they were not only wonderful, but highly improbable. Not to dwell upon many incidents relating to himself which he foretold, I consider the destruction of Jerusalem, which our blessed Lord so exactly described, as one of the highest and most incontestible proofs of his possessing this divine attribute in its full extent. The destruction both of the city and the temple; the signs and wonders which should precede these events; the calamities which should ensue; the dispersion of the Jewish people; nay, the very ensigns of the nation, by whom the destruction was to be effected; all are related with a precision surpassing credibility, in a mind merely human, and can only be resolved into the infinite knowledge of him, to whose observation, the past, present, and future, are but as the same object. One part of this memorable prophecy of our Lord remains yet to be fulfilled. And the same prescience which predicted the dispersion of Israel, could not err in the assurance that they should again be gathered in. A day will come when "the Deliverer will arise from Zion, and turn away ungodliness from Jacob," (Rom. xi. 26.) May the Lord hasten this glorious event, and bring on that promised day of grace when "a little one shall become a thousand, and a small one a strong nation!" (Isaiah lx. 22.)

† See Sermon II.

"which had glory with the Father before the world," and "without whom was not any thing made that was made," must have been himself "without beginning of days, or end of life." But to put the matter beyond all dispute, our blessed Lord confirmed the whole when he appeared to his beloved apostle, in that glorious vision mentioned in the Book of the Revelations; and called himself by these divine titles, which can only be applied to an Eternal Being, "I am Alpha and Omega, the First and the Last," (Rev. i. 8, 11.)

Immutability is another peculiar and distinguishing attribute of GODHEAD; and if the testimony of an apostle be valid, we cannot forbear ascribing it to the person of Christ. "Jesus Christ (says he) the same yesterday, to-day and for ever," (Heb. xiii. 8.) Terms which need no explanation. The same apostle, in another place, speaking of the eternal and unchangeable nature of Christ, draws a striking contrast between him and his works. "Thou, Lord, in the beginning hast laid the foundation of the earth, and the heavens are the works of thy hands; *they* shall perish, but *thou* remainest, and *they all* shall wax old as doth a garment, and as a vesture shalt thou fold them up, and they shall be changed; but *thou* art the same, and thy years shall not fail," (Heb. i. 10, *et seq.*) These are strong expressions of the immutability of the divine nature; and there can be no doubt to whom the whole refers, if we consult the original.

Omnipotency is another peculiar character of the Deity. And nothing can be more clearly applied to Christ. All the works of Creation, Providence, Grace, and Judgment, are declared to be his. As all things are said "to be made by him, so by him do all things consist." "He upholdeth all things by the word of his power." "He is able to subdue all things to himself." He it is, who is "full of grace and truth," out "of whose fulness have all we received, and grace for grace."

The resurrection and the life, at "whose voice all that are in their graves will come forth," and by whose power all will be raised to judgment at the last day, "when the Lord Jesus shall be revealed from heaven with his mighty angels." His mighty angels! how fully descriptive of sovereignty and power! And who can behold such an assemblage of qualities uniting in the person of our glorious LORD, and constituting every idea we can form of omnipotence, and still question his claim to GODHEAD?

Holiness is so distinguished an attribute of the Godhead, that perhaps it is this, more eminently than any other, which draws the line of separation between the divine and human nature. And this is also ascribed to Jesus. He is not only called *Holy*, but by way of emphasis the *Holy One*, (Acts xiii. 35.) And the prophet Daniel, in describing the future events of the Messiah's kingdom, makes use of the same appellation, the *Most Holy*, (Dan. ix. 24.) In the Apocalypse, our blessed Lord is revealed under the same exalted character: "These things saith he that is holy, he that is true," (Rev. iii. 7;) as if this phrase was applicable only to himself.

From the *attributes* let us pass on to examine the *names* by which Jesus Christ is no less distinguished in scripture, and we shall find the same invariable testimony arising from hence of his divinity. In short, both titles and attributes, and all the peculiar and distinguishing properties and perfections of the Godhead, which are in one part or other fully ascribed to the person of our Lord, all concur to justify his own assertion, when he said, "All things that the Father hath are mine," (John xvi. 15.)

Some of the names and titles by which Christ is known in scripture, have been incidentally noticed in what hath been already offered. It will be the less necessary, therefore, to be particular. I shall produce a few instances sufficient to answer the present purpose.

It is well known that the highest and most eminent distinction by which the Father is revealed in his holy word, is the incommunicable name of the great JEHOVAH. This, indeed, is so peculiarly his own, that it can be applicable to none but the self-existing and independent God. Now this very term we frequently find made use of when speaking of the person of our Lord Jesus Christ. For the most part, the word *Jehovah* in the Old Testament is the same as *Lord* in the New. And had the original been preserved, this would have been more manifest. In the Old Testament, the great Jehovah is said to be the only Saviour over all the earth. "Look unto me, and be ye saved, all the ends of the earth; for I am God, and there is none else; I, even I, am the Lord, and beside me there is no Saviour," (Isa. lxv. 22, xliii. 11.) In the New Testament, the same character is preserved, and the correspondence shown. St. Peter explains this very passage of the prophet, and applies it to our blessed Lord, when he says, "Neither is there salvation in any other; for there is none other name under heaven given among men whereby we must be saved," Acts iv. 12.

The prophet Jeremiah clearly defined the person of our Lord, when he proclaimed the Messiah under that distinguishing name, *Jehovah our Righteousness*. For Christ alone is *our Righteousness*, according to the apostle, and "wisdom, and sanctification, and redemption," (1 Cor. i. 30.) And the prophet Zechariah, when, speaking in the character of Jehovah, he says, "they shall look on him whom they have pierced," could mean no other than *him* whom the apostle John declared was pierced by the soldier on the cross, that this "scripture might be fulfilled.*

* Compare Zechariah xii. 10, with John xix. 37.

You will not expect me to enumerate all the passages with which the word of God abounds, in proof that the incommunicable name of the great Jehovah is frequently made use of when speaking of the person of our Lord. This would be unnecessary. I shall dismiss the consideration of it, therefore, with only observing, that when we behold this sacred distinction of the self-existent and uncreated Being, thus repeatedly, and without hesitation applied to Christ, nothing can more clearly imply his Godhead. For he "whose name is Jehovah (as the Psalmist justly observes,) can only be the Most High over all the earth," (Ps. lxxxiii. 18.) And when to this we add how exceedingly scrupulous the Jews were of using this hallowed name, lest they should incur the penalty threatened to the taking it in vain; it cannot be supposed the apostles, who were all of them Jews, and bred up in Jewish notions, would have been forward in ascribing it to our Lord, but upon the most perfect conviction of its being right. And, therefore, we may very safely adopt the words of the apostle Peter, "Let all the house of Israel know assuredly, that God hath made that same Jesus which was crucified, both Lord and Christ," (Acts ii. 36.)

Another term of distinction by which our blessed Lord is frequently mentioned in scripture is that of *God.* The prophet, when declaring the advent of the Messiah, said, his name shall be called the "Mighty God," (Isa. ix. 6.) And the apostles of Christ have confirmed it. St. Paul calls Jesus the "Great God," (Tit. ii. 13.) "God our Saviour," (Tit. i. 3;) and "God over all, blessed for ever," (Rom. ix. 5.) And, speaking of *his* church, he declares it to be the church of the "living God," (1 Tim. iii. 15.) St. John, to the same amount, styles Christ the true God: "this is the true God, and eternal life," (1 John v. 20,) alluding, perhaps, to our Lord's account of himself, when he says, "I am the resurrection and the life." And St. Jude, in his epistle, terms him "the only wise God our Saviour," and ascribes to him all divine honours. "To the only wise God our Saviour, be glory and majesty, dominion and power, now and for ever," (Jude 25.) All which very strongly express the Godhead of him to whom they applied, and are such characters as cannot possibly be ascribed to any inferior being.

Nor are these all. Christ is yet further known in his holy word, under other titles of a like exalted nature. He is said to be "the Lord of glory, which none of the princes of this world knew; for had they known it, they would not have crucified the Lord of glory," (1 Cor. ii. 8.) He is declared to be the "Lord of all," (Acts x. 36;) and St. Peter, in his sermon to Cornelius, and his company, called him by this name. But more particularly the beloved apostle hath left on record such testimonies of his divine LORD, in those revelations with which he was favoured, as leave no room to question the Godhead of his person. More than once he heard a voice proclaim him under that almighty character, "King of kings, and Lord of lords," (Rev. xvii. 14, 19, 26;) than which nothing can more fully shew his power and greatness. And it is remarkable that in the same chapter in which it is said, that "Jesus sent his angels to testify these things in the churches," it is also said, that it was "the Lord God of the Prophets that sent his angel;" a plain proof that "Jesus is the Lord God of the Prophets," (Rev. xxii. 6.)

And to sum up all, our blessed Lord closes the sacred canon of scripture with this testimony of himself: "I am Alpha and Omega, the First and the Last. I am he that liveth, and was dead; and behold, I am alive for evermore, and have the keys of hell and death," (Rev. xxii. 13.) This solemn declaration was made to the apostle by one whom he saw like the *Son of man*, the well-known character of our blessed Lord. Indeed, had the person not been specified, the words themselves would clearly have ascertained to whom they belonged. None but Christ could have said, "I am he that liveth, and was dead, and behold, I am alive for evermore." And to leave the full impression of those glorious truths on the minds of the faithful, he repeats the same assurances of his eternity in the conclusion of the visions. "I am Alpha and Omega, the Beginning and the End, the First and the Last." All which are parallel to the declarations God is pleased to make of himself, by his servant the prophet: "I am the First and the Last, and beside me there is no God," (Isa. xliv. 6.)

Now, then, consider the united evidence arising from the attributes and names by which Christ is every where distinguished in the holy scripture. We find the same, or equivalent phrases applied both to the Father and the Son, and from this equal participation of all the perfections of the Godhead what can we possibly infer less than the GODHEAD of Jesus? Is not this what Christ means, when he says to his Father, "All mine are thine, and thine are mine?" (John xvii. 10.)

Besides, is it possible for any man to believe the sacred writers would all have concurred in speaking of the person of Jesus under such eternal distinctions, by which alone the great Sovereign of the universe is known to his creatures, unless they had received the most perfect conviction of it? For it should be observed, that those attributes and titles of Jehovah are not ascribed to our Lord in one or two passages only, and of a doubtful nature; but in numberless instances, of the clearest and most obvious meaning, and scattered over every part of the apostolic writings. Supposing, then, it were possible to be mistaken in the application of any single part of our evidence, yet this ought not, it cannot, indeed, affect the whole. The clear proof of our Lord's possession of any one of the eternal perfections ascribed to him, must determine at once the certainty of his divinity. And to imagine that such a body of evidence should arise in scripture, testifying as to a matter of fact what was yet questionable, would be childish in the extreme. It would be to suppose the sacred writers were either ignorant themselves of the real character of Jesus; or, what is, if possible, yet less to be believed, were perfectly indifferent what consequences might follow their testimony. Nay, more than this, that God himself should suffer a spirit of delusion and error to make its way into the church, instantly on its establishment, and continue its baneful influence through so many ages from the days of the apostles to the present hour; which is at once the most senseless, not to say ungodly idea that can be conceived. And yet the conclusion seems inevitable on the presumption that our Lord is not truly divine. In short, the evidences are so numerous and diversified, in support of this great article of our faith, that the want of belief is not to be accounted for on common principles, and can only be ascribed to what holy scripture hath stated: "If our Gospel be hid, (saith Paul) it is hid to them that are lost; in whom the god of this world hath blinded the minds of them which believe not, lest the light of the glorious Gospel of Christ, who is the image of God, should shine unto them."*

* 2 Cor. iv. 3, 4. I cannot prevail upon myself to close this view of the Redeemer, under those exalted characters, in the united testimony to his deity, from the attributes and appellations by which he is described in scripture, without subjoining a short note, by way of carrying additional conviction to any unbelieving reader into whose hands these feeble discourses may come; and also to point out what resources of comfort such views of Jesus ought to afford to all his faithful people.

I would first desire the man who hath not yet received sufficient evidences to satisfy his understanding of the divinity of Christ; but yet whose mind is not absolutely shut against *all* conviction, only coolly and dispassionately to review once more what hath been brought before him in the course of this Sermon, concerning our Lord's possession of all divine attributes, and those eternal distinctions of character by which he is known. Let him ask himself this single question, whether it be possible to suppose that a Being can be distinguished by such incommunicable properties, to be present at all times, and in all places, "upholding all things by the word of his power;" his *eye* unremittingly directed to take in with one comprehensive glance, every object both in heaven

But what raises the character of Jesus to the highest point of sublimity is, that important purpose which is declared by the sacred writers to be the great end and design of his mission; I mean, "the taking away sin by the sacrifice of himself," (Heb. ix. 26.) This implies a superiority in his nature distinct from all former prophets or teachers of mankind, and which, from very evident causes, could never be accomplished by any being merely human. And hence the prophet, who proclaimed our Lord's approach, and became the herald of his appearance, pointed to Jesus under this remarkable character, "Behold, the Lamb of God, which taketh away the sin of the world," (John i. 36.)

---

and in earth; his *ear* open to the numberless cries of all creatures; his *arm* stretched forth to support, restrain, protect, punish, and reward the various subjects of his providence: and all this to millions and millions of creatures, in one and the same moment; and yet all the while be a created being, or the delegated creature of another? Oh! the absurdity of modern infidelity! What contradictions will it not reconcile rather than bow down to the truth. Reader! whoever thou mayest be, who art tainted with this spirit, think, I charge you, before it be too late, how awful the case of those who die in unbelief. "If ye believe not that I am, (says Christ) ye shall die in your sins," (John viii. 24.) Grant, Lord, the power of believing! take away all hardness of heart from this people: open every blind eye; and unstop every deaf ear; that we may not be any longer "rebellious, or turn away backward."

But for you who are his believing people, contemplate, I charge you, in those gracious perfections of your Redeemer, what a rich provision you possess in Him for all you need. Recollect, moreover, that all the dispensations, both of providence and grace, are his. Not a sparrow can fall to the ground but by his appointment: nay, the very hairs of your head are all numbered. In his hands all your concerns are safe. "He hath the keys of David. He openeth, and no man shutteth: he shutteth and no man openeth." Oh! what an inexhaustible resource have all true believers in Christ, under every dispensation both of sorrow and of joy, in the perfections and merciful designs of their Redeemer! Keep up, I beseech you, an unceasing attention to him, ye that are his believing people, in all the events of life; and learn to make the same personal and practical application of all the chequered circumstances of a transient existence, which the apostle did for himself and his faithful companions in the gospel: "I am persuaded (says he) that neither death, nor life, nor angels, nor principalities, nor powers, nor things present, nor things to come; nor height, nor depth, nor any other creature shall be able to separate us from the love of God which is in Christ Jesus our Lord," (Rom. viii. 38, 39.)

It would be departing, in some measure, from the more immediate object of my discourse, to go over all the evidences we have in Scripture, respecting the great doctrine of atonement; and yet I cannot content myself without observing, that it is this, of all others, which peculiarly distinguishes the Christian faith.

Independent of all the authority we derive from holy writ, it is a fact which remains not now to be disputed, that forgiveness of sins has been the great object mankind in all ages have stood in need of; and sought after with the most anxious solicitude, to calm the fears of an awakened conscience, when smitten with the sense of guilt. The heathen world, long before the coming of Christ, had the most lively apprehensions of what sad consequences *might* follow the sins of this life, and studied by every mean in their power to prevent them. Hence they had recourse to every offering superstition could invent, to propitiate the offended Deity. The religion of the Jews partook much of the same nature. By expiatory sacrifices, they were led to hope some compensation was made for the breach of moral duties. And as these were of divine appointment, though the human mind could trace no affinity between the slaughter of a beast and the sin of a man, yet it seemed to soothe the conscience with the hope of pardon.

Now, whether or not what the apostle to the Hebrews hath asserted, will be admitted, that "these were shadows of good things to come, of which the substance was Christ," (Heb. x. 1, 9;) yet one thing is certain, this universal consent to expiatory sacrifices plainly shews the great anxiety of the world on this important point: and it is but a fair conclusion, that if God were pleased, in compassion to his sinful creatures, to make a further revelation of his will, after the many ineffectual attempts which had been made by his servants the prophets to bring mankind from ways of sin to paths of virtue; and that another more powerful messenger should come on this grand embassy; he would at least satisfy the mind of man concerning the means of propitiation, and shew wherein the efficacy of the offerings appointed under the law did consist. For to suppose otherwise, by leaving mankind in the dark on this interesting topic, would be to suppose the gospel still defective in that part particularly, which most materially concerned the wants of our nature.

But if Christ came to teach a system of moral virtue only, and no more, alas! this had been done before. Moses had done it. Many prophets and righteous men had done it. But to what effect? It was not mere precept and example that could restore human nature to its original purity. Neither was it the calling upon sinners to return to the Lord, which gave them the power of returning. This would have been like bidding a man who was chained down to the earth with bars of the hardest iron, to burst asunder the bands of his own accord, and rise up and walk. Supposing, therefore, that Christ came only to answer this purpose, wherein did his commission differ, or in what point was it superior to that of Moses? And could it be an object worthy a messenger from heaven to deliver a law of righteousness which had been so ineffectually delivered more than a thousand years before, and to preach the same doctrines which had been so repeatedly preached in vain? Is it possible, that any man can seriously think that God would deal thus with his poor, fallen, and helpless creatures? Let reason answer the question (for to this great arbiter I here appeal for the decision), whether this would have been either to the honour of God or the advantage of man?

When you have duly pondered the force of this argument in favour of the great doctrine of atonement, go on and review the evidences for the fact itself.

The prophets had predicted, that "the Messiah should be cut off, but not for himself: that he should make his soul an offering for sin: that by his righteousness he should justify many, and bear their iniquities." In conformity to this, when our blessed Lord came into the world, he declared himself to be this very sacrifice, and that the end of his mission was for this express purpose. "I am the good Shepherd: the good Shepherd layeth down his life for the sheep."* And in his discourses he frequently made mention of his death, sometimes in a figurative way, and at other times more openly; but always as an event of the utmost importance to mankind, and as the great end of his ministry. "I am the living bread which came down from heaven, if any man eat of this bread he shall live for ever; and the bread that I will give is my flesh, which I will give for the life of the world. The hour is come that the Son of Man should be glorified: verily, verily, I say unto you, except a corn of wheat fall into the ground and die, it abideth alone; but if it die, it bringeth forth much fruit," (John xii. 24.) And as the time approached nearer, Christ expressed himself more openly concerning this great event. "Now is my soul troubled; and what? shall I say, Father, save me from this hour; but for this cause came I unto this hour," (John xii. 27.) And when discoursing with his disciples at one time upon the interesting subject of his mission, he in plain terms declared to them, that his death was purposely appointed as a sacrifice for sin. "The Son of man came not to be ministered unto, but to minister, and to give his life a ransom for many," (Matt. xx. 28.) To give his life a ransom for many! What could this imply, but that he was to be an expiatory offering? When do we find any moralist, any of the old prophets or messengers from God, talk in a language like this? Surely these expressions must evidently prove that some higher purpose than merely instructing mankind was included in the

* Compare John x. 11, with Isaiah liii. and Dan. ix. 26.

ministry of Jesus, and that his death was more particularly to be considered also in the nature of an oblation and atonement for sin!

Nor is this all the evidence that Christ gave respecting this doctrine. The institution of that solemn supper which he appointed as a standing ordinance in his church, implied the importance of the object it was intended to perpetuate. The bread which was to be broken, and the cup to be poured forth, were altogether emblems void of meaning, if the death of Jesus be considered in the light of a martyr only to his cause. But viewed as the memorial of an oblation for sin, they then become apt and significant representations of his body, which was broken, and his blood, which was shed, for "the sins of the world." And hence the apostle justly reasons, "the bread which we break, is it not the communion of the body of Christ? The cup of blessing which we bless, is it not the communion of the blood of Christ?" (1 Cor. x. 16.) The communion of the body and blood of Christ is a strong expression, and clearly intends something more than the commemoration of his death. To have a full idea of it, let us only suppose it had been said of any of the apostles, that, in a service of this kind, it was called the communion of *their* body and blood! and the ungodliness of the application will be immediately glaring.

But it is not only on the authority of Christ himself, great and unquestionable as that authority ought to be, that we ground the certainty of this doctrine. The apostles, also, after their being endued with the influence of the Divine Spirit, in all their discourses inculcate the same thing. The writings of those inspired men abound with phrases of the plainest kind in proof of it. One assures us, that Christ "died for our sins according to the Scriptures," (1 Cor. xv. 3;) that "we have redemption through his blood, even the forgiveness of sins," (Ephes. i. 7;) that "he made our peace through the blood of his cross," (Coloss. i. 20;) and that "he gave himself a ransom for all," (1 Tim. ii. 6.) Another declares, that "Christ bare our sins in his own body on the tree," (1 Pet. ii. 24;) that "we are not redeemed with silver and gold, but with the precious blood of Christ, as of a lamb without blemish, and without spot," (1 Pet. i. 18, 19.) A third proclaims, that it is "the blood of Christ which cleanseth from all sins," (1 John i. 7;) and that "he is the propitiation for our sins," (1 John ii. 2.) And all concur in asserting, that the great end of our Lord's coming was, to "put away sin by the sacrifice of himself." Are all these mere words without meaning? If so, how comes it to pass that such things should be said of Jesus only, and not of any former messenger of God? Do we discover any expressions of a similar tendency in any of the writings of the prophets? Was it ever said of Moses or Elijah, or any other holy servant of God, that they took away sin by the sacrifice of themselves?

And, as if all these were not sufficient to confirm the certainty of the doctrine, it is further remarkable, that when the apostle John, in a vision, saw heaven opened, and heard the acclamations of the happy multitude; this, he tells us, was the universal chorus of praise and thanksgiving, which he heard, "Thou wast slain, and hast redeemed us to God by thy blood," (Rev. v. 9.) All which, if language can be depended upon, decidedly prove, that the first and leading principle of the gospel, is the atoning blood of its blessed Author. And it is not without the strongest evidences we conclude, that Christ is to us a sacrifice for sin, as well as an example of a godly life. But I pursue this reasoning no further. Suffer me only to assume the possibility of the fact itself, that "we are sanctified through the offering of the body of Jesus Christ," (Heb. x. 10,) and the superiority of his nature must immediately be admitted. For to give efficacy to that oblation, it became expedient that he should be "holy, harmless, undefiled, separate from sinners," (Heb. vii. 16,) and in every way untainted with the pollution of that fallen race whose guilt he suffered to expiate. And hence, therefore, must be inferred the GODHEAD of his person.

The evidences in proof of this important doctrine, which arise from the last scenes of our Lord's history, though carrying with them a peculiar energy, are of a nature much easier to be conceived than expressed. In the plain and unaffected narrative of the Evangelists, it is impossible, under grace, not to feel their impression. The awful signs which they relate as accompanying the death of Jesus, and the glorious manifestation which attended his resurrection and ascension; altogether proclaim a dignity in the person of our Lord, infinitely transcending all ideas of a being merely human; especially when it is considered that Christ had foretold every remarkable circumstance which distinguished those events. He had declared, indeed, not only that his death was voluntary, but that his resurrection should be the result of his own immediate power. "No man taketh my life from me, but I lay it down of myself. I have power to lay it down, and I have power to take it again," (John x. 18.) "For as the Father hath life in himself, so hath he given the Son to have life in himself. And as the Father raiseth up the dead, and quickeneth them, even so the Son quickeneth whom he will," John v. 20, 21.) And hence it was that Christ said to the Jews, "Destroy this temple, and in three days I will raise it up. But he spake" (the Evangelist tells us) "of the temple of his body. When, therefore, he was risen from the dead, his disciples remembered that he said this unto them," (John ii. 19, *et seq.*)

But on these topics I forbear to enlarge. They possess an energy in the words of the Evangelists perfectly inimitable, and which cannot but suffer under a representation from all other pens.

One evidence, however, of Christ's GODHEAD resulting from the view of the conclusive scenes of our Lord's life, is so very pointed, that I venture to propose it to your more particular consideration; namely, the unequalled dignity which they have given to our Lord's person and manner, during his last interview with his apostles; and the authority with which he delivered to them his final commission.

" He had shewn himself alive to them after his passion by many infallible proofs, being seen of them for forty days, and speaking of the things pertaining to the kingdom of God," (Acts i. 3); and having " opened their understanding, that they might understand the Scriptures," and shewed them the expediency on which it was founded, that " thus it was written, and thus it behoved Christ to suffer, and to rise from the dead the third day," (Luke xxiv. 45, 46;) he now proceeded to deliver to them that commission which involved in it all the great events of his church. " All power is given unto me in heaven and in earth. Go ye, therefore, and teach all nations, baptizing them in the name of the Father, and of the Son, and of the Holy Ghost. And lo, I am with you alway, even unto the end of the world," (Matt. xxviii. 18, *et seq.*) " And these signs shall follow them that believe. In my name shall they cast out devils; they shall speak with new tongues; they shall take up serpents; and if they drink any deadly thing, it shall not hurt them; they shall lay hands on the sick, and they shall recover," (Mark xvi. 17, 18.) " And he led them out as far as Bethany, and he lifted up his hands and blessed them. And it came to pass, while he blessed them, he was parted from them and carried up into heaven. And they worshipped him, and returned to Jerusalem with great joy," (Luke xxiv. 50.) " And they went forth and preached every where, the Lord working with them, and confirming the word with signs following. Amen." (Mark xvi. 20.) What grandeur and sublimity are there in these words! What a concurrence of circumstances to illustrate and prove the divinity of our blessed Lord! With an authority unequalled he dismisses his humble followers to the arduous enterprise of the conversion of a world, assuring them at the same time of his continual presence! And in the proof of the high commission under which they acted, they were to carry the fullest evidences with them of his divine power. In *his* name they were to cast out devils, and perform all their mighty works. And accordingly, when they went forth upon their employment, it is said, "the Lord was working with them, and confirming the word with signs following." Are not these very high demonstrations of the GODHEAD of Jesus? Did ever any character among the sons of men assume a language like this? or had ever any one his pretensions justified by the correspondence of events so singular? I ask not what prophet or messenger of God acted in this manner; but I demand, what angel from heaven ever claimed such distinctions, or mentioned his own name as the efficient cause of his ministry?

But this is not all. The apostles before they proceeded to preach the Gospel, were to receive supernatural assistance to qualify them for the work in the descent of the Holy Ghost; and even this, Jesus declared, should be his own immediate gift. When the Comforter is come whom I will send unto you from the Father, even the Spirit of Truth which proceeded from the Father, he shall testify of me," (John xv. 26.) "He shall not speak of himself, but whatsoever he shall hear that shall he speak, and he will shew you things to come. He shall glorify me, for he shall receive of mine and shall shew it unto you. All things that the Father hath are mine, therefore said I that he should take of mine, and shew it unto you, (John xiv. 13, *et seq.*) Is it possible to hear these things, and still question the GODHEAD of him by whom such declarations are made? That Christ should say of the blessed Spirit "which searcheth all things, yea, the deep things of God," (1 Cor. 10,) and whom "to speak a word against is pronounced to be unpardonable sin," (Matt. xii. 32); "that when the Comforter is come whom I will send, he shall not speak of himself, but he shall receive of *mine*, and shew it unto you!" Can we conceive it possible that any being less than the great Supreme should talk thus freely of the Holy Spirit? And that the Holy Spirit should actually descend upon the minds of the apostles in perfect conformity to those declarations of Jesus?

Nay, more. The form of baptism which our Lord appointed for the introduction of converts into the Gospel-covenant, and which is become the grand charter of the church, is yet, if possible, more difficult to be accounted for upon the supposition that his GODHEAD be denied. When Christ sent his disciples into all the world to preach the Gospel to every creature, the command was, "baptize them in the name of the Father, and of the Son, and of the Holy Ghost," (Matt. xxviii. 19.) In which form Jesus classes himself in priority of rank, before the Eternal Spirit, and separates, as it were, between the Father and the Holy Ghost. Was this without design, and without meaning? Had our Lord no object in view in doing it? I should suppose this impossible. And what then are we to conclude, that any created being, however high or exalted, would be so presumptuous as to place himself on a level with the Father, and the Divine Spirit? What could be more blasphemous, or derogatory from the honour of God! Surely the advocates for the simple humanity of Jesus must, upon their own principles, suppose that our blessed Lord far exceeded his commission by thus encroaching upon the divine prerogatives; for it is impossible to assign any reason for his assuming this equality, unless it were his right. And, for my own part, I cannot but observe, that this form of baptism, (which is evidently the solemn dedication of Christians to God in the name of the Father, Son, and Holy Ghost) would of itself be more than half conviction with me of the divinity of our blessed Master, even if unsupported by the other direct testimonies of holy Scripture.*

One point more remains yet to be considered, by which the dignity of the great Author of the Christian faith is clearly ascertained, namely, the supreme character in which he is to appear as the Judge of the world.

The Scriptures have so fully and plainly revealed the doctrine of a future judgment and a day of account, that it forms a part of every man's creed, and is the common object of universal expectation. That our blessed Lord is to preside at this awful tribunal, is an opinion also in which all Christians are agreed, though

---

* The form of baptism, if considered with all its attending circumstances, carries with it a peculiar evidence in proof of the GODHEAD of our Lord. The great Author of our faith had lately suffered death upon the cross, for the *supposed* blasphemy of calling himself the Son of God. In this solemn interval of his resurrection and ascension, when he was delivering his final commission to his disciples, concerning the future events of his church, and at the time when he had received "all power in heaven and in earth;" can it be supposed that if any misconception had been taken, either of his person or doctrine, from what himself had taught, he would not have embraced this favourable season for correcting their error? More particularly in so momentous a point, as that of entertaining right notions of his person and character, would he have left them in ignorance whether he was really and truly what he had all along professed himself to be, the Son of God, and for which he had suffered death, or had assumed this title only by way of distinction of character? Instead of this, or any explanation to a similar effect, what are our Lord's final declarations? Truly, the fullest confirmation of his "unity with his Father," in the appointment of a solemn service by which the converts to the faith were to be initiated into the Christian communion, in the joint name of the Father, of the Son, and of the Holy Ghost; what conclusion can possibly be made of it, but an equal participation of GODHEAD? When we recollect the numerous passages of Scripture, which ascribe divinity to each of the sacred persons of the Godhead, and then behold Christ in the instance before us, as enjoining all his followers to be baptized in the equal profession of this faith, from which no tribulation whatever was deemed to be a sufficient justification for receding; the appointment and form of this service become, I conceive, a very decisive evidence of the great point in question.

the divinity of his person is by some rejected. But certainly the exercise of supreme authority but ill corresponds with the notion of a subordinate being. The very description which the sacred writers have given of this "great day of the Lord," is enough to impress the mind with the fullest conviction that there must be somewhat truly divine in his person and character, who possesses a sovereignty so supreme. When we read, that "the Lord Jesus shall be revealed from heaven with *His* mighty angels in flaming fire, taking vengeance on them that know not God," (Thess. i. 7); that "he cometh with ten thousand of *His* saints, to execute judgment upon all," (Jude 15); and that "the very heavens and earth will flee away from the face of *Him* who sitteth upon the throne," (Rev. xx. 11.) Are these things credible upon the supposition that Christ is no more, after all, than an human being? Is the belief of it consistent with principles of common sense?

Again, our blessed Lord, in his predictions of this day, declared that "all who are in their graves should hear his voice and come forth;" but is it to be the voice of a glorified man which is to effect this? to rouse the dead, to re-animate the lifeless mass of dust and ashes, and to abolish for ever the empire of death and the grave? Can this be really possible? But what is still more astonishing, (and which the rejecters of our Lord's Godhead must receive with unreserved conviction,) is the opinion, that this man, Christ Jesus, in consequence of his exaltation, possesses such an intimate knowledge of the human heart, with the infinite circumstances and transactions of life, as to be able to determine the exact measure of duty or disobedience in every man's conduct; and can draw the line of strict justice with the nicest hand, so as to ascertain the rewards and punishments due to every individual of the innumerable race of Adam. Can any one seriously and coolly adopt this opinion?

Let us for a moment, however, pass the boundaries of probability, and in opposition to the numberless obstructions in the way, let it be admitted. Now, then, we reduce in idea the great Judge of all the earth to the humble standard of humanity. But even here again a new difficulty arises. To what cause can we reasonably ascribe this wonderful exaltation? What was there in the life of Jesus, simply considered as a man, which merited this astonishing accession to the right-hand of power, to be the Judge of quick and dead, and to determine the everlasting fate of millions? I speak with all possible reverence, and even with a religious apprehension upon my mind, while proposing questions of this bold nature. But surely, it could never be merely for preaching a system of moral virtue, or being a pattern of the most perfect righteousness, much less for dying as a martyr to his cause, and sealing the testimony of his doctrine with his blood. These are very inadequate causes, wherefore "a name should be given to him which is above every name," (Philip. ii. 9.) Great as these characters are in themselves, and surpassing all comparison with those of the highest and best of men, yet is there no proportion between the merit and the reward: it is without parallel, in all the dispensations of Providence that have ever been revealed to mankind.

But now, consider the subject in another point of view. Suppose this spotless preacher and example of righteousness, to be literally and truly what the sacred writers have declared him to be, the Son of God, and possessed, as himself hath assured us, of "glory with his Father before the world;" then, for the purposes of our salvation, and in mercy to a fallen race, conceive him descended from this state of felicity, clothed in a body of flesh, in that form offered a sacrifice upon the cross for human guilt; and, having accomplished this important end, suppose him returned to his original glory, whence he will come again at the last day, agreeably to his promise, to judge the subjects of his moral government.

Beheld in this light, nothing appears disproportioned in the Gospel dispensation; but one uniform scheme of infinite wisdom, blended with justice and mercy. The strictest propriety is visible in *his* being the Judge of mankind, who hath been their Creator and Redeemer. And though, no doubt, the highest mystery is veiled under a dispensation so awful, yet we see enough to admire, and in that admiration to adore, the gracious ordination of heaven in this last, best, and *unspeakable gift*, 2 Cor. ix. 15.

What true believer, in a review of those proofs of divine love, can refrain from joining the apostle in his animated exclamation: "O the depth of the riches both of the wisdom and goodness of God! how unsearchable are his judgments, and his ways past finding out! For who hath known the mind of the Lord, or who hath been his counsellor? For of him, and through him, and to him, are all things: to whom be glory for ever, Amen." (Rom. xi. 33—36.)

SERMON VII.

MATTHEW XVI. 15.

But whom say ye that I am?

THE numerous and unexceptionable evidences of scripture in favour of our Lord's GODHEAD, have now, in a very circumstantial manner, been brought before you. The subject has been traced through the whole of the sacred writings, (and I hope free from prepossession or partiality) in order to ascertain the real character of our glorious GOD and Saviour! And I would willingly persuade myself, that the result of the inquiry hath terminated in impressing your mind with the clearest conviction that *Jesus* is the *Son of God.*

To these testimonies there seems nothing further necessary to be added, except it be the opinion of the first and immediate followers of Christ, his apostles. It becomes, indeed, a very material and important question, in the final decision of the whole argument, to inquire what were the sentiments of these holy and inspired men upon the subject. For their opinion is of the greatest consequence, and must carry with it considerable weight with every candid mind. And if it can be shewn (as I think it may without much difficulty) that they entertained a perfect persuasion of the GODHEAD of Jesus, I should apprehend there ought to be no hesitation in adopting their sentiments and taking them for our pattern, in subscribing to this great article of our faith.

That it was the *general* opinion of those faithful servants of Christ, (as far as we are able to gather from their words or writings,) hath been, in a great measure, proved from the occasional quotations which, in the course of these Sermons, have been already made. But on a point of so much consequence, it may not be amiss to examine, somewhat more distinctly, the *particular* opinion of each of them.

The investigation of this subject will require your present attention.

The question in the text appears to me to be the most suitable to this purpose; " But whom say ye that I am?" It was originally proposed by our Lord himself to his disciples on this very point. Whether Christ intended it altogether for the trial of their faith, or whether he meant that their opinion might become the standard and guide to succeeding ages of the church on this grand question, I shall not determine; yet I cannot but think there is something very remarkable, both in the manner of our Lord's interrogating his disciples upon it, and the observations he made in consequence of Peter's answer. For, after Christ had gathered from them the general sentiments of mankind concerning his person and character, he then desired to know, what was *their* opinion upon the subject. When *Simon Peter*, for himself and his brethren, said, " Thou art Christ, the Son of the living God;" had we any doubts what the apostle meant by this expression, the observations which our Lord made upon Peter's answer would immediately remove them, by determining the sense in which he considered it. " Blessed (says Christ) art thou, Simon Barjona, for flesh and blood hath not revealed it unto thee, but my Father which is in heaven." If Peter meant nothing more by these words, than that he and his fellow-apostles considered Jesus as a *servant*, or *messenger* from God; surely Christ would not have pronounced him to be blessed for the confession; for multitudes, who knew but little of our Lord's character, more than from seeing the miracles he daily wrought, confessed the same thing. " A great prophet (say they) is risen up among us, and God hath visited his people," (Luke vii. 16.) Neither would the discovery have been so very remarkable and important, that flesh and blood could not have attained to it, but it must have proceeded from the immediate revelation of God, if, at the same time, it amounted to nothing higher than the belief that Christ was simply a *man*, and differed not from any former prophet, except in the extent of his commission. To me, I confess, it appears one of the plainest propositions possible, that Peter (and of consequence his fellow apostles with him,) intended by the expression to profess his belief that our Lord was a being of that superlative nature, and so intimately united to God, as to be his *Son;* and that Christ considered the apostle's words in this sense, and pronounced a blessing upon him for the profession of such a faith.*

This passage serves to give us some idea of the *general* opinion of the apostles concerning the person and character of their blessed Master. But the object I proposed from the present discourse was, to learn (as far at least as the holy Scriptures can inform us) what was the *particular* sentiment of each of them on this momentous point, separately and individually.

Before I proceed to this, however, it may be proper to premise a few words respecting the validity of their opinion.

When we consider the number, the situation, and the character of the apostles, it is impossible to suppose that they could be under the influence of a delusion

* There is somewhat so very gracious in those divine words of the LORD JESUS to Peter; namely, that the revelation of the Person and GODHEAD of CHRIST could not be the effect of human power in all its highest efforts; and only from the FATHER; that I cannot but beg the reader to ponder them well. And when we see in life, as that we daily do, men of the first abilities in human arts and sciences, alive to the quickest apprehension in all earthly concerns; but as blind as beetles, if you only touch on spiritual concerns; what a confirmation doth this daily give to our LORD's words! Oh! the unspeakable felicity of being taught of GOD! (Isa. liv. 13; John vi. 45.)

themselves, or capable of joining in a confederacy, with a view to delude others.

The humble prospects of Christ's religion favoured no such idea, nor was there any object they could have proposed to themselves to have been answered by it. They had, no doubt, at the first, in common with their countrymen the Jews, many prejudices to vanquish previous to their becoming sincere believers in our Lord's character as the Messiah. And we find it was necessary that evidences, again and again, should be brought before them to accomplish this purpose. Therefore, the establishment of their own conviction became necessary, before they could be supposed qualified to attempt the conviction of others. So that when we hear one of them declare, that the truth of the facts they delivered was, "what they had seen with their eyes, what they had looked upon, and their hands had handled of the word of life," (John i. 1,) we may very safely conclude, that as they could have no inducement whatever to deceive the world, so neither is it credible that they could have been deceived themselves.

But this is not all. Their opinion is still more highly deserving our reverence and regard, from the supernatural assistance which they are well known to have received, in order to qualify them as witnesses of the great truths of the gospel.

The promise of this divine aid was given to them by Christ himself before his departure. And it was declared by him, among other purposes, to be one grand reason for which he left the world, that he might "send them the blessed Spirit of truth, which should guide them into all truth," (John xvi. 13.) But indeed, not only from the authority of Scripture do we derive the testimony of the inspiration of the apostles, but our reason confirms the certainty of it, by the strongest evidence. For how should a few poor, ignorant fishermen of Galilee, dull, and unlearned even to a proverb, as they were, undertake upon their own strength, the arduous enterprise of converting a world to the doctrine of a crucified Redeemer? If we consider them, indeed, as endued with power from on high, every difficulty at once vanishes. Supported by this divine aid, all opposition must fall before them; and their testimony thereby, becomes the greatest and most convincing that is possible. That divine *Spirit of truth*, which was promised "to guide them into all truth," would not, we may be assured, leave them ignorant respecting so important a point as that of the real character of their LORD: especially as their testimony would become the great standard of faith with sincere believers to the latest ages of the church. So that we may, without the least hesitation, place an implicit confidence in their opinion, and be convinced that those *holy men of God*, in all that relates to the person and doctrines of their Lord, "spake as they were moved by the Holy Ghost," (2 Peter i. 21.)

This being premised, I proceed now to the grand question, What were the sentiments of those servants of Jesus concerning the real character of their Master?

The testimony I shall begin with, is that of *John the Baptist*, whose early ministry claims this precedence. This man was not an *apostle* of Christ, indeed, but being his fore-runner, may very properly be classed among the servants of our Lord. His evidence is the strongest that can be, and we shall have a better conception of it, if we previously consider the high terms in which he is spoken of in holy Scripture. It was said of him, by the angel who predicted his birth, that "he should be filled with the Holy Ghost, even from his mother's womb," (Luke i. 15.) And the Evangelist St. John says, "that he was sent from God for a witness, to bear witness of the light, that all men through him might believe," (John i. 7.) A witness from God surely challenges a more than ordinary attention from man! And, as if these relations of John were not sufficient to impress our minds with the strongest conviction of the greatness of his character, our Lord himself sums up the account when he says, that "among them that are born of women, there hath not arisen a greater than John the Baptist," (Matt. xi. 11.) Indeed, there was somewhat so singular and striking about the person of John, that when he began his ministry, "all men mused in their hearts whether he himself were not the Christ," (Luke iii. 15.) Such was the eminence and sanctity of John the Baptist! Let us hear, therefore, this man's testimony concerning our blessed Lord.

He opened his commission by preaching the doctrine of repentance as the necessary means for "preparing the way of the Lord;" and in all his discourses constantly referred to *him* that was to follow him. And that no question might arise whose way it was that he prepared, the apostle Paul, in his sermon to the Ephesians, hath determined the matter. "John (says he) verily baptized with the baptism of repentance, saying unto the people, that they should believe on him which should come after him, that is, on Christ Jesus," (Acts xix. 4.) And when the Jewish Sanhedrim, in consequence of this new doctrine, and the multitudes that flocked from all parts to hear John preach, sent priests and Levites to demand who he was, and whether he were the Christ, he disclaimed all pretensions to that high title, and modestly assumed to himself the office only of being his forerunner. "I am the voice (says he) of one crying in the wilderness, Make straight the way of the Lord, as said the prophet Esaias," (John i. 23.) It were unnecessary, I should suppose, to observe, that the prophet Isaiah, when predicting the Messiah's approach, (in his fortieth chapter) literally described his Harbinger under this exact character. One part, however, of this prophecy (and that a most essential part in proof of the doctrine we are now treating of,) I must desire may be attended to with that particular and respectful notice to which it is entitled by its great importance; namely, that this voice, which it was predicted should cry in the wilderness, was to prepare the way of the Lord: not the way of a *man*, however great or distinguished; but "the way of the Lord;" to make straight in the desert, "an highway for our God:" that then the glory of the Lord was to be revealed, and all flesh should see it together.* Admitting, therefore, what has never been disputed, that John the Baptist was he whom the prophet had in view in this memorable prophecy, which the Evangelists declare, and our Lord himself confirms;† nothing can more fully define the dignity of *his* sacred person, whose way he came to prepare.

And that John considered Christ in this exalted point of view, is evident from the account he gives of himself when compared to him. "I, indeed, baptize you with water, unto repentance, but one mightier than I cometh, the latchet of whose shoes I am not worthy to stoop down and unloose; he shall baptize you with the Holy Ghost," (Matt. iii. 11.) What humiliating notions must this "greatest among them that are born of women" have entertained of himself; and what unequalled ideas of his divine LORD, the very "latchet of whose shoes" he thought himself "unworthy to unloose!" Is it possible he could have expressed the GODHEAD of Jesus in stronger terms than these?

Again:—The day after John had given his answer to the question of the Priests and Levites, he repeated his testimony of our Lord, with other more particular marks of distinction; for, seeing Jesus coming towards him, he saith, "Behold the Lamb of God, which taketh away the sin of the world! This is he of whom I spake, After me cometh a man which is preferred before me, for he was before me," (John i. 29, 30,) evidently alluding to our Lord's pre-existence; for, with respect to

* See Isaiah xl.

† Compare the Evangelists *in loco* with Isaiah xl.

the appearance of Christ in the flesh, John was born six months before him, and therefore he could not have said this, but in reference to his former being. But what renders the Baptist's testimony so highly conclusive and important, is the assurance he gives, that all his knowledge of Jesus was derived from supernatural information he had received. That, as to himself, he was totally ignorant both of the nature and dignity of Christ, until these things were confirmed to him by the corresponding tokens which attended the baptism of Jesus, and which he who had called him to the office of an herald, pointed out as the distinguishing marks by which he should know the Messiah: "I knew him not, (says he) but he that sent me to baptize, the same said unto me, Upon whom thou shalt see the Spirit descending, and remaining on him, the same is he which baptizeth with the Holy Ghost. And I saw, and bare record, that this is the Son of God," (John i. 33, 34.)

Such is the testimony of John the Baptist on the important question of our Lord's GODHEAD. After the review we have taken of his evidence, it would almost be an insult to the understanding, to demand what must have been the opinion of the Baptist concerning the person of Christ. For surely it is impossible to suppose, that he could have ascribed to our Lord so many distinguishing properties of a divine Being, but under a perfect assurance of his divine nature. When, therefore, we recollect that one principal object of John's embassy was for a "witness to bear witness to the truth, (John v. 33,) that all men through him might believe," (John i. 7,) his single testimony ought to have more weight than a thousand arguments, to strengthen and confirm the faith of believers in this great article of our religion. And though, as our blessed Redeemer hath himself observed, "he hath greater witness than that of John, (John. v. 36,) and receives not testimony from man," (John v. 34,) because, in fact, he needs it not;

yet to us, it becomes a very strong collateral consideration, in addition to the numerous evidences with which this principle of our faith is every where supported in the sacred writings. And, as I am well assured, the testimony of the Baptist cannot but be highly gratifying to every sincere believer in the divinity of Jesus; so I hope this man's evidence who came, let it be remembered, " a witness to the truth, that all men through him might believe," will be seriously and coolly considered by every one who may be in danger of being led away by a different persuasion, before this grand and distinguishing article of the Christian church is relinquished.*

---

* In the conclusive scenes of John's life, a circumstance occurs which has been thought by some to favour a different opinion from what the Baptist had given before of our Lord. As one whose duty and inclination both prompt him to candour, I think it highly proper to produce it upon the present occasion, but without the smallest apprehension that it will be found, when duly considered, to militate against John's former testimony, but rather strengthening it. The circumstance I allude to is, the question which John sent, when in prison, by two of his disciples, unto Jesus, saying, " Art thou he that should come, or look we for another?" If we attend to the context we shall find, that John sent this message at a time when his disciples brought him intelligence of the mighty works of our Lord. And as these were so many additional proofs of Jesus answering to the character John had given him, it cannot be supposed the account of them would lessen the Baptist's opinion of Christ. It would be very extraordinary, that he, who had given the most decided evidence to the greatness of our Lord's character, and whose evidence sprung from somewhat more than human authority, should afterwards have scruples of his own to satisfy, and now, in the end of his ministry, should begin to doubt the truth of our Lord's mission. It has been said that, perhaps the mind of John, soured by long imprisonment and unjust suffering, might be warped from his former sentiment. Perhaps it might. No doubt, the pressure of trouble may induce effects of this kind. How weak is the faith of the best of men very frequently found under severe trials. How often are sincere Christians tempted to exclaim in the anguish of their soul, " Hath God forgotten to be gracious?" When they know, and are convinced in the same moments, that the Lord is very gracious. Suppose somewhat like this to be the situation of John, his sufferings might have given an asperity to his temper, and yet his notions of Christ might continue just the same. But I do not see the necessity of supposing John had any doubts in his mind concerning our blessed Lord, when he sent his disciples with this message unto him. I rather think the whole design of

From John the Baptist, let us proceed to Peter the Apostle, whose opinion concerning the character of Christ, must be equally acceptable, and together with it become of great weight in the argument.

That our Lord was of a divine nature, and differing most essentially from a mere man, in the sentiments of Peter, can hardly be questioned, from the several quotations of Scripture which we have already taken notice of; for such declarations as the apostle occasionally made, during the life of Jesus, cannot possibly be reconciled with a different opinion. Hence we hear him frequently expressing his faith, that "Jesus is the Christ, the Son of God." But it is not barely assenting, in so many words, to this truth, that we consider as the only criterion of his judgment; for we find him also, testifying his belief by a corresponding behaviour, as one that had the fullest persuasion of our Lord's GODHEAD. Once, indeed, as if in a dependence upon it, attempting, at the command of Jesus, to walk upon the water, which plainly implied an unbounded confidence in the power of Christ, (Matt. xiv. 28.) Such conduct is not to be accounted for, upon principles of common sense, with the supposition that all this while Peter believed his Master to be no more than a mere man, and in every respect the same as himself, except in the commission he had received from God.

But there are circumstances yet more pointed to indicate the sentiments of Peter, during some particular occasions, in the life of Christ. As for example, in his

---

the Baptist was with a view to *their* conviction, and not *his own*. The disciples of John felt, perhaps, a laudable concern at the growing popularity of our Lord, and the decline of their master's reputation. John had endeavoured to convince them, that "he was not the Christ, but only sent before him," (John iii. 28.) In order, therefore, to satisfy their scrupulous minds concerning the dignity of Jesus, the Baptist adopted this method of introducing them more immediately into our Lord's presence, that from seeing and hearing the wonderful effects of his ministry, they might be convinced that he was the Messiah which was for to come. (John iii. 30 to the end.)

retirement on the mount, when only Peter, and James, and John, were permitted to be present with him, and when our Lord was transfigured before them; the glory, or shechinah, in which he then appeared, was so similar to the glory of Jehovah, on Mount Sinai, that it produced the same effect upon the apostles as that did on Moses, for "they feared as they entered into the cloud," (Luke ix. 34.) And it was this resemblance, no doubt, which suggested to the mind of Peter the idea of building three tabernacles, on which the glory might remain, as it used to do upon the tabernacle in the wilderness.* But the most remarkable circumstance in this awful scene, is the effect the voice, which came out of the cloud, produced upon the apostles, in declaring our Lord to be "the beloved Son of God;" for when they heard it, they fell upon their faces and "were sore afraid." What sentiments the apostles entertained of their Lord, in consequence of this solemn transaction, is not, indeed, expressly said; but if their behaviour can be supposed to imply any thing, it gave the most positive assurance that they were deeply smitten with the consciousness of the greatness of his character. And had they desired to shew their perfect apprehension of the presence of the GODHEAD, they could not have done it more emphatically than by prostrating themselves to the earth as they did before Christ, and continuing in that situation until the vision was past.

Another incident in the life of Jesus, where the

---

* It is impossible for the most ordinary reader to peruse the account of this scene of Christ's transfiguration, and compare it with the relation that is given of the descent of Jehovah on Mount Sinai, without being struck with the wonderful resemblance between them. The glory in which Jehovah was encircled, the cloud covering the mount, the apprehension of Moses as he entered into the cloud, all are exactly similar to the description of the transfiguration; I think myself justified, therefore, in supposing that it was the recollection of the history of this solemn scene, which put into Peter's mind the idea of the Jewish tabernacle. (Compare the Evangelist *in loco*, with Exodus xxiv. 15. *et seq.*)

apostle Peter appears to have had the most lively sense of the GODHEAD of his LORD, was shewn at the miraculous draught of fishes. The behaviour of Peter upon this occasion seems to have arisen from a religious apprehension upon his mind, such as we read in Scripture affected holy men of old, when under a consciousness of the divine presence. Of this kind was the dread Jacob felt on seeing the face of God at Peniel, (Gen. xxxii. 30;) and of Gideon and Manoah, upon the appearance of an angel, (Judges vi. 22, xiii. 22.) The words which Peter made use of, in consequence of the wonderful capture of fishes, can only be explained upon the same principle. Convinced by this act of our Lord, that there was somewhat of a superior nature in his person, and fearing, after such a display of divine power, what other effects might follow, "he fell down at the knees of Jesus, saying, Depart from me, for I am a sinful man, O Lord," (Luke v. 8.)

These occurrences during the ministry of our Lord, afford very strong arguments to the persuasion, that Peter, as well as the other apostles, occasionally considered their blessed Lord under a character very different from that of a mere man. I say, *occasionally;* for it should be observed, that it is not during the season in which our blessed Lord continued among them, that we are to look for their full attestation of Christ's divinity. Their faith was then imperfect and wavering; their notions of Jesus, crude and undetermined. It was a long time before they could be brought to relinquish their national prejudices, which had taught them to expect a mighty prince, and a deliverer, in the person of the Messiah, so as to receive our Lord under that character. Nor, indeed, was the conviction, that "it was he that should deliver Israel," (Luke xxii. 21,) firmly rooted in their minds, until the great events which followed the death of Jesus in the coming of the HOLY GHOST, had corrected their judgment respecting the nature of the

Messiah's kingdom, and thoroughly instructed them, in what related to the great object of his mission.

The writings of the prophets, in their predictions of the promised Saviour, had, it is true, fully shewn that some mysterious union would constitute his character; and that he should be both a suffering and a triumphant prince. Yet it were a weakness to suppose, that a body of ignorant fishermen should be so well read in Scripture as to comprehend what even the Sanhedrim could not explain. Hence, therefore, it is not during the life of Jesus, that we are to expect from the mouth of the apostles a settled and undeviating testimony to his GODHEAD. The expressions leading to this opinion, which we find they occasionally made use of, are rather to be considered as given in some peculiar moments, when the rays of his divine nature bursting through the veil of flesh in which he was clothed, forced a transient conviction from his astonished disciples; but which the familiar occurrences of a few days soon again effaced. Similar to the common effects of the world. Some of the most splendid operations, however powerfully they may awaken the faculties of the mind, yet they produce only a momentary impression, which the recurrence of familiar objects very speedily removes. Somewhat of this kind was the situation of the apostles, with respect to the opinion they were prompted to entertain of their Lord's divinity. They beheld numberless events in the life of Jesus, which plainly declared him to be more than mortal. His words, his actions, his miracles, in short, every occurrence connected with his more immediate ministry, were altogether great and illustrious; yet when viewed in conjunction with the common circumstances of a man, and of a very poor and humble man too, can we wonder that such things should frequently banish from the memory of the disciples the real greatness of their Lord's character? To repeat, therefore, what was just before observed, we are not to look for a fixed opinion on this great question from the disciples, until the descent of the Holy Ghost. When, indeed, this divine illumination from above had fully informed their minds of the principles of the gospel, and they were qualified to become witnesses unto Christ, "both in Jerusalem and Judea, and Samaria, and to the uttermost parts of the earth," (Acts i. 8;) then may we expect to find, in all the accounts they give of the person and character of their Lord, one uniform and steady opinion. And such, I conceive, to have been the general sentiments of the apostles upon this important question; bearing, upon every occasion, as far as was expedient, with the leading object of their commission, a full evidence to the GODHEAD of CHRIST.

In particular, Peter, whose testimony we are now considering (and who holds so distinguished a rank among the apostles), hath left us sufficient information, both from his discourses and his writings, to conclude, that after being enlightened with the influences of the Holy Spirit, he was but the more strongly confirmed in the sentiments he had before occasionally entertained of the divine nature of Christ.

Whoever examines his first sermon, preached on the day of Pentecost, with an unprejudiced mind, will perceive strong marks of the perfect conviction which Peter must have possessed of this great truth. But in that critical season, when addressing a body of Jews upon the subject of our Lord's mission and character, it certainly required no small degree of caution, how he insisted much upon so delicate a point as the GODHEAD of one whom they had lately crucified. It is worthy of observation, what discretion the apostle used upon this occasion, so as to engage the attention of his audience, and no less to remove their prejudices against the doctrine he was anxious to recommend. He begins his sermon, therefore, by appealing to their own knowledge, for the truth of the wonderful events which had distinguished the life of Jesus of Nazareth, "a man (says he) approved of God among you, by miracles and wonders, and signs, which God did by him, in the midst of you, as ye yourselves also know," (Acts ii. 22, *et seq.*) And to obviate any ill effects which might arise in their minds, from the recollection of the part they had acted in the death of Jesus, he declares that his death was entirely brought to pass "by the determinate counsel and foreknowledge of God;" and that, in consequence of this divine ordination it was, "that they had crucified and slain him." Having thus guarded against what was most likely to have inflamed their minds, had the apostle mentioned these truths with the smallest acrimony; he now proceeds to the great object he had in view, from his discourse, namely, to assert the certainty of our Lord's resurrection; and (what is most to my present purpose) he does this by proving that this glorious event was accomplished from physical necessity; or to use the stronger expression of the apostle, "having loosed the pains of death, because it was not possible that he should be holden of it." If these terms do not imply the apostle's persuasion of the divine nature of our Lord, I am at a loss to comprehend any meaning in them. For had Peter considered Jesus but as a man, nay, had he not considered him above the nature of a man, there was no impossibility in the thing itself, of his being holden by what he calls "the pains of death." And, as a further confirmation of this doctrine, he brings before them the prophecy of David, and applies it to the person of Christ. "For David (says he) speaketh concerning him, I foresaw the Lord always before my face; for he is on my right hand, that I should not be moved. Therefore did my heart rejoice, and my tongue was glad; moreover also my flesh shall rest in hope: because thou wilt not leave my soul in hell, neither wilt thou suffer thine Holy One to see corruption." Having quoted this passage, Peter desires permission to speak freely upon it, and calls upon them to observe, that these things could have no reference to the Patriarch David, because "he was both dead and buried, and his sepulchre remained unto that day: but being a prophet, and knowing that God had sworn with an oath, that of the fruit of his loins, according to the flesh, he would raise up Christ to sit upon his throne: he seeing this before, spake of the resurrection of Christ, that *his* soul was not left in hell, neither his flesh did see corruption." By these arguments, having proved the physical necessity of the resurrection, both from our Lord's nature, and the concurrent testimony of prophecy, the apostle, in the conclusion of his sermon, describes the Redeemer under such expressions as carry with them the most satisfactory proofs, how strongly impressed his mind must have been with the belief of the superior nature of our Lord. "Therefore (says he) let all the house of Israel know assuredly, that God hath made that same Jesus, whom ye have crucified, both Lord and Christ."

In Peter's second, and subsequent sermons, he names our Lord by such titles as would be the highest ungodliness, if applied to any created being. He calls him the Holy One, and the Just, the Prince of Life, (Acts iii. 14, 15.) And when we find that the preaching of Peter was accompanied with such demonstrations of *his* power, under whose commission he acted; miracles both of mercy and judgment, purposely wrought to establish the faith, and all expressly done in the sole name, and by the power of Jesus Christ; is it reasonable to suppose, that the apostle should thus preach, and act, and constantly refer all the glory to his blessed Lord, and yet have no apprehensions of his GODHEAD? That he should work every miracle as by *his* authority, and proclaim every blessing to be expected, but through *him:* nay, to declare, that salvation could be through no other; "neither is there any other name under heaven given among men whereby we must be saved," (Acts iv. 12:) and still all this while believe that Jesus was simply no other than a man like himself; and that it was the merit of a man only, through whom salvation for millions of the human race could be procured? Can it be possible to suppose this? Surely it requires such a stretch of credulity, as the highest mystery of the Christian faith cannot be charged with, to give into the belief of such a persuasion! Be the matter of fact, therefore, whatever it may, concerning the real dignity of our blessed Lord, that Peter had a conviction of his divinity cannot, I think, well be doubted, for the contrary notion would be hard to reconcile with those repeated declarations we meet with in his discourses.

Before we quit our review of this man's evidence, it may not be amiss to add, that as in his preaching, so in his writings, we find his testimony the same. In his last epistle (written as is very probably supposed,* the year before his martyrdom, and at a time when he had the prospect of death in view; and purposely written, that they who had obtained like precious promises with himself, might be able, after his decease, to have the truths of Christianity always in remembrance in this epistle); he shews very plainly, that as he had lived, so he died, in the faith of this important doctrine. The apostle, among other matters, particularly alludes to the glorious scene of Christ's transfiguration; and the observations he makes upon it, may serve to convince us, what impression it had left upon his mind of the greatness of his Lord's character. "We have not followed (said he) cunningly devised fables, when we made known unto you the power and coming of our Lord Jesus Christ, but were eye-witnesses of his majesty. For he received from God the Father, honour and glory, when there came such a voice to him from the excellent glory, This

* It is with great reason imagined, that Peter wrote his Second Epistle, anno 67; and history informs us, that he suffered martyrdom anno 68, the fourteenth year of the Emperor Nero.

is my beloved Son, in whom I am well pleased. And this voice which came from heaven we heard when we were with him in the holy mount," (2 Pet. i. 16, *et seq.*) Enough hath been said, I should hope, in the introduction of particulars to ascertain what was the opinion of the apostle Peter concerning the person of Jesus Christ. And if I have faithfully stated this man's testimony (which I trust I have), his evidence is such an one, as (to use his own words) "we shall do well to take heed unto, as unto a light that shineth in a dark place," 2 Pet. i. 19.

The same observation with which I began the review of Peter's testimony, may, with equal propriety, be made respecting the evidence of the apostle John. After the plentiful quotations from the writings of this disciple, any further reference is unnecessary, in order to shew what were his sentiments upon the subject of Christ's deity. Indeed the very preface to his gospel is in itself a full decision of it. Without going over his writings again, suffer me only to detain you with one observation more, respecting the evidence of this highly favoured servant of his Lord, which will supersede the necessity of many lesser arguments; and that is, the account which he has given of the supreme dignity of Jesus, in his book of the Revelations. In this mysterious canon of Scripture, we find much information concerning our Lord's real character, which might be produced with great advantage to our present cause; but a single passage will be sufficient. In the first chapter the apostle, after opening his subject with the highest ascriptions of praise and dominion, "to him that loveth us, and hath washed us from our sins, in his own blood;" goes on to describe the personal appearance of our Lord to him, in an effulgence of brightness and glory, in which Jesus assumes every divine honour, and speaks of the future dispensations which were to take place in his church. What sentiments the apostle then had, and ever after retained, concerning the GODHEAD of CHRIST, let any one who reads John's account of this vision determine. "When he saw him (he says) he fell at his feet as dead," and heard him proclaim his name under these great characters, "the Alpha and Omega, the First and the Last." Could he possibly doubt the GODHEAD of such a being? Did the apostle consider these eternal properties belonging to our Lord, but as so many distinctions of the glorified man Christ Jesus? And at the time when he was under the immediate impression of this vision, or afterwards when he recorded it for the edification of future ages, had he no apprehension himself that Jesus was any thing more than a man, whom God had highly exalted for the perfect merit of his life, and his beneficial ministry; and yet with not the least idea of the divinity of his Lord, he should transmit such accounts of him as must determine others to the belief of it with perfect conviction? Are such palpable contradictions to be admitted? Strange, that it should not immediately appear to persons of this opinion, that they are not only impeaching the veracity of John as a writer, but bringing the heaviest accusation against the great Saviour of the world, in suffering such representations of him to be made in his church, as must infallibly lead into error the faith of mankind! Could we but once suppose this, the blessing which is promised "to him that readeth the words of this book, and keepeth the things which are written therein," (Rev. i. 3,) would be converted into a curse; and unable to satisfy the mind with the certainty of any one proposition we meet with in Scripture; we should be like the dove of Noah in search of land, without a place to rest our foot on through the whole of God's word. Praised be the Divine Goodness, the matter is not left to a reasoning so precarious and uncertain! "The disciple which testifieth of these things, and wrote these things," could not be deceived; "we know that his testimony is true," (John xxi. 24:) "for these things were written that we might believe that Jesus is the Christ, the Son of God, and that believing we might have life through his name," (John xx. 31.)

The evidence of Thomas the apostle, on the great question of our Lord's GODHEAD (which is the next to which I request your attention), is so decisive upon the subject, that it hath with great reason been considered as one of the most important testimonies upon record. Even they who reject the belief of Christ's divine nature, are yet at a loss to reconcile their different opinion with this man's sentiments. It is but a single incident in the life of Thomas, in which we find this profession of his faith, and delivered upon a memorable occasion; but it is an incident which hath proved (as no doubt it was designed by the providence of God) the most favourable and propitious to the establishing the minds of believers firm and unshaken, in this great article of their creed.

It is, I believe, generally known, that the absence of Thomas from the first assembly of the disciples, after our blessed Lord arose from the dead, prevented that sight of Christ, which would most probably, had he been present, have produced the same conviction upon him that it did upon the rest. But though there seems to have been no apparent reason, wherefore he should doubt the truth of the report of the resurrection of Jesus (considering the assurances he had received of the fact itself from his fellow apostle), yet, from an unaccountable incredulity, Thomas not only refused to believe it upon their testimony, but also declared that he never would be convinced of it, but upon such evidence as appeared at that time highly improbable should be granted him.

Upon the next meeting, however, of the disciples, Thomas was present with them, and in a manner similar to his former visit, Jesus again appeared before them. His miraculous entrance,* and his immediate address to

* The miraculous entrance of our blessed Lord amidst the circle of his disciples, is so very high a proof in my esteem of the deity of his nature, and so important to my present argument, that I must desire to

the unbelieving disciple, in offering the very proofs he had demanded for his conviction, so powerfully operated upon the mind of the apostle, in confirming both the certainty of his resurrection, and the divine power by which he had accomplished it, that subdued by these evidences, he cried out in an ecstacy of joy, "My Lord! and my God!" Though no form of words could more strongly express the divinity of him, to whom it was applied, yet it hath been said, that this confession of the apostle's was simply no other than the effect of a sudden surprise, as if he had said, "Then it was really true!" But never was there a more miserable expedient to get rid of a difficulty.

Had the words of Thomas been merely an excla-

---

insist up it somewhat more particularly. Sceptics have been pleased to bring forward this account of Christ's interview with his apostles, with great confidence as making against the credibility of the fact itself, of the resurrection of Jesus. Unable to account upon philosophical principles for the entrance of a body into a room when all the avenues were shut by which any thing substantial might pass; they have been pleased to treat the whole as fabulous. But so far is the thing itself from giving just occasion to this cavil, that the impossibility of accounting for it upon physical principles, proves the very point in question, namely, that it was accomplished by the divine power of Jesus. It is indeed a full proof of our Lord's omnipotency. For that Christ effected this entrance by means truly miraculous, is evident from the circumstances of the case. In the evangelist's account of it, it is remarkable that he is no less particular in his observation that "the doors were shut," than he is in stating the certainty that it was the "real body of Christ" which appeared. He tells us that Jesus pointed out to his disciples the difference between a spiritual essence and a material substance, that "a spirit had not flesh and bones as they saw he had:" and in testimony that what they saw was real, "he shewed them his hands and his side," and desired they would yet further convince themselves of the truth of it by feeling him. All which fully prove, that the disciples were not under the influence of an illusion in what they beheld, but that it was the real body of Jesus which had been crucified. Now as the entrance of a body into a room, as before described, could not have been accomplished but by some supernatural agency (it being contrary to all the known properties of physics), it must follow that He who possessed the supreme power of altering or suspending at his pleasure the established laws of nature, possessed also omnipotency, which can belong only to God.

mation of astonishment, how comes it to pass that Christ should have considered them as the profession of his faith? For there is a manifest difference between wonder and conviction. And yet it is plain, that our blessed Lord accepted what Thomas said, as the confession of the fullest conviction; "Because thou hast seen me, thou hast believed." Besides, had Thomas spoken as a man under the immediate effect of surprise, and without any particular meaning, it is not likely that he would have done it in so deliberate and repeated a manner. He might have said, *My Lord!* or *My God!* singly, but not both. The uniting of these expressions, should not seem very probable in the apostle's circumstances, nor do I think, that in this case, Thomas would have addressed himself so immediately to Christ, as it is evident he did, but rather to the disciple that happened to be nearest to him. But whether these considerations are to the purpose or not, there is one which certainly is, namely, that in the original the article which is prefixed invariably determines the sense, wherever it is used with those words, as being applicable only to God. It is therefore wholly unaccountable that the apostle should address Christ in those words, unless he had a real apprehension of the GODHEAD of his person. And to suppose otherwise, that Thomas, though using such expressions, had no conception of Christ's divine nature, would be still more unaccountable, and our Lord's conduct equally mysterious. To call him *Lord and God*, whom he considered in the very moment of saying it but as a *man*, became idolatry. And yet we hear of no reproof from Jesus for the expression. Christ indirectly blames him indeed for his *former* incredulity, but not a word for his *latter* error. Whereas the one was infinitely more reprehensible, (supposing it to be misapplied) than the other. And that Christ should be altogether inattentive to this conduct in his servant, which, from his omniscience, he could not but be sensible would be of great moment in succeeding ages of the church, as a standard of faith to the believer, is the most unlikely circumstance that can be imagined. In short, whoever can reconcile these points to his own satisfaction, so as to reject the testimony of Thomas to the divinity of our Lord, possesses a degree of credulity not very enviable. But he who will fairly and impartially consider the several circumstances connected with this incident in the life of the apostle will, I think, perceive strong leading characters to induce the persuasion that Thomas could not but have the most complete conviction that Christ was GOD.

The next testimony which I have to produce is of equal consequence with the former, for it was given in a peculiar situation, even in his dying moments. You will perceive I allude to that of Stephen. This man was not in the general acceptation of the word an apostle. He was, however, a disciple of Christ, and what is more immediate to our subject, he may be said to have died a martyr to the very profession of our Lord's GODHEAD.

His evidence is briefly related in the sixth and seventh chapters of the Acts of the Apostles, where we read that the zeal of Stephen for the faith of the gospel, having inflamed the minds of the adversaries to Christianity with anger, they suborned men to accuse him "of speaking blasphemous words against Moses, and against God." The blasphemy against Moses is particularly specified, in that he said, "Jesus of Nazareth would destroy the temple, and change the customs which Moses delivered." But what could be the blasphemy against God? What was there in the doctrine of the apostles which could possibly bear this construction, except that of ascribing divinity to our blessed Saviour? The apostles had never ceased to observe among themselves, and to recommend to others, every known duty which the law enjoined to God the Father: and it is impossible to discover any thing in their conduct which could be deemed blasphemy, unless it be the divine honours which they paid to the person of Jesus. That this was Stephen's crime there can be but little doubt. For it is observable, that notwithstanding the rage of his enemies against him, they heard the holy man with great patience, through a long address which he made before the council, while he recited the principal heads of the Jewish history. And, most likely would have granted him a longer audience, had he not connected with it the relation it bore to our blessed Lord; but no sooner did he advert to the name of Jesus, and distinguish him by the title of the Just One, (the well-known character of GODHEAD) declaring them to have been his *betrayers* and *murderers*, than "they gnashed upon him with their teeth." In this critical moment, "Stephen, being full of the Holy Ghost, looked up steadfastly unto heaven, and saw the glory of God, and Jesus standing on the right-hand of God. And he said, Behold, I see the heavens opened, and the Son of man standing on the right-hand of God." Confirming in this open and avowed manner, the testimony which he had before borne to the divinity of Jesus, they were unable to suppress their resentment any longer; but, "crying out with a loud voice, and stopping their ears, they ran upon him with one accord, and cast him out of the city, and stoned him," while he with his dying breath recommended his departing soul, not immediately to the Father, but to Christ: "Lord Jesus, (says he) receive my spirit." Whether this profession of Stephen was the cause of death, I shall not insist upon; but one thing is very evident; if this man did not die a martyr to the GODHEAD of Christ, he at least died in the faith of it. And in either case, the conclusion to our present argument is the same. Such a testimony to this great article of our faith, from one under the full influence of the Holy Ghost, is peculiarly satisfactory, and cannot but impress the mind with a very strong weight of evidence.

I shall close our review of the opinion of the apostles

concerning the character of Jesus, with the testimony of St. Paul, who, though with great humility, he styles himself " the least of all the apostles, and not meet to be called an apostle, because he persecuted the church of God," (1 Corinth. xv. 9,) yet, in the estimation of his LORD, he was " a chosen vessel, to bear his name before Gentiles, and kings, and the children of Israel," (Acts ix. 15.)

Added to the inspired character of St. Paul, let us recollect, that he was converted to Christianity by a miracle from heaven, and after his conversion, the gospel which he preached, he solemnly affirms before God, he " neither received of man, neither was taught it by man, but by the revelation of Jesus Christ," (Gal. i. 11, 12.) A more unexceptionable witness can never be desired.*

You have already noticed, I hope, in the many quotations which have been brought before you, from the Epistles of this man, what exalted accounts he has left upon record, of his Lord's character. And as these views of Christ, according to the apostle's opinion, clearly ascertain a superior dignity in his nature, it becomes a very natural question, from whence could Paul have acquired this information concerning Christ? Before his conversion, it is certain he could have had no such notions of the character of our Lord; for he was a violent persecutor of the Christian faith, and held both the name and religion of Jesus in hatred and derision. And after that miraculous event took place, it is said of him, that he conferred not with any one upon the subject of Christianity, but " straightway he began to preach Christ in the synagogue, that he is the Son of God," (Acts ix. 20.) It is too fabulous to suppose, that the apostle

* If Paul neither received it by *man*, neither was taught it by *man*, and yet had this knowledge by the revelation of Jesus Christ; can any thing be plainer than that the apostle considered Christ as more than *man?*

should be led by an intuitive kind of knowledge in himself, to entertain those sublime ideas of Christ, especially after his former opinion of him; and if it be true that he received not this information from man, neither was taught it by man, there can be no reason to reject the solemn assurance he has given, that it was communicated to him by the revelation of Christ himself. And hence it will follow, that if our Lord condescended to be Paul's instructor, after having called him, even at the expence of a miracle, to be his servant, and giving him all necessary information respecting himself and his religion, there can be nothing erroneous in his account; and we may, with great safety, receive his testimony as infallible, for no human authority can equal it. When, therefore, we trace through every part of his inspired writings an invariable strain of evidence to the divinity of Jesus, and every great and distinguishing attribute which constitutes GODHEAD, applied to the person of Christ, can it be the question of a moment, what were the sentiments of the apostle Paul concerning his divine LORD?

But in reply to these arguments, we are told that our interpretation of these passages of the apostle, arises from a misapprehension of his meaning: that he wrote in accommodation to the spirit of the language then in use, which was very highly metaphorical and flowery, and therefore a great part of his expressions is to be considered in this sense. These things have been said and much insisted upon, but with what strength of argument comes next to be considered.

In Paul's First Epistle to the Corinthians, he tells them that when he came to them preaching the gospel, "he came not with excellency of speech, nor was his preaching with enticing words of man's wisdom, but in demonstration of the Spirit and of power," (1 Cor. ii. 1, 4.) "For we use (says he) great plainness of speech," (2 Cor. iii. 12.) And so he does indeed, upon the presumption, that we are to accept what he says, according to the most natural meaning which it bears; but if we are to look beyond the first sense of the words, and fancy one part to be mysterious and another figurative; how will this agree with the apostle's declaration, that "he uses great plainness of speech?" St. Paul, it is true, calls the sublime parts of the Christian faith a mystery, and says, "Great is the mystery of godliness: God was manifest in the flesh," (1 Tim. iii. 16.) But when he said this, he evidently alluded to the mystery of the incarnation: whereas if he meant nothing more by it, than that Jesus Christ was but a *man*, what *mystery* was there in this scheme of *godliness*, and how could this be called "God manifest in the flesh?"

Again: It is somewhat remarkable, that Paul should caution Timothy, as he does, to "withdraw himself from men of perverse disputings and corrupt minds:" and to remark, moreover, that "if any man consent not to wholesome words, even the words of our Lord Jesus Christ, and to the doctrine which is according to godliness, that he is proud, and knowing nothing, but doting about questions and strifes of words," (1 Tim. vi. 3, 4, 5.) All this is very singular in coming from a man who is supposed to be continually wrapping up his instructions, not in wholesome words, but in allegory and figure; and yet who, at the same time, declares the great cause of the rejection of the gospel, is from the pride and wisdom of the world, to whom "the preaching of the cross is foolishness," (1 Cor. i. 18.)

It is still more remarkable, that in this apostle's Epistle to the Colossians, he bids them "beware lest any man should spoil them through philosophy and vain deceit, after the traditions of men, after the rudiments of the world, and not after Christ;" and in the next verse, immediately adds, "for in him dwelleth all the fulness of the Godhead bodily," (Col. ii. 8, 9.) Had the apostle feared he should be misunderstood in this passage, instead of telling the Colossians, to beware of the "traditions of men," and the "rudiments of the world," he should have warned them against supposing that he meant any thing by the "indwelling of the Godhead bodily in Christ;" whereas, there is not a syllable said of this, but only a caution against being spoiled by that "philosophy and vain deceit," which prompt men to cavil with such truths of religion as are not fairly upon a level with the apprehensions of the human mind.

These considerations serve to explain, in what sense we are authorized to accept the writings of Paul; and to suppose that a man, who professedly used great plainness of speech himself, and recommended it to others, should dwell so continually in figure as to mislead the understanding of his readers upon all occasions.

But besides those instances, which we have reviewed in proof of the apostle Paul's testimony to the divinity of Jesus Christ, there is one more which remains to be noticed, equally decisive, and which can upon no consideration whatever be explained, but upon the belief that the apostle had a full persuasion of the GODHEAD of our Lord; I mean the prayers which he offered up personally to Christ.

The awful scene in the road to Damascus, at the time of his conversion, is the first instance of the kind we meet with in Paul's history, in which he addressed our Lord, and received an answer to his petition, (Acts ix. 6.) And again, we find the same application immediately made to Christ when the apostle was under some particularly afflicting circumstance, for which he says, "he thrice besought the Lord that it might depart from him," (2 Cor. xii. 8.) That it was Christ, and not the Father he prayed to, is evident from the whole affair as related. And it should seem indeed, both from this incident, and from various accounts to be traced in his writings, that it was the apostle's usual custom in his devotions, immediately to address them to the Lord Jesus Christ. He inscribes his Epistle to the Corinthians, not only *to them*, but " to all that in every place call upon the name of the Lord Jesus," (1 Cor. i. 2.) And his general benediction, with which he concludes his Epistles, implies the same: " Grace to you and peace from God the Father, and from the Lord Jesus Christ."

I fear I have exhausted the patience with which you have hitherto heard me on the present subject. But the testimony of the apostles, and first servants of Jesus, concerning the real character of their LORD, became too interesting, to be hastily passed over, and without due examination.

The several opinions of those " chosen witnesses of God," have now been brought before you (as far as they are obtainable;) and when you have thoroughly reflected upon the evidences themselves, and the fair and unimposing manner in which they have been offered to your consideration; you will give them, I doubt not, the credit to which they shall appear to you to be justly entitled.

The whole question respecting the validity of their testimony may be reduced to a single point. Either they were believers in the divinity of Jesus, or they were not. If they were *not*, I shudder at the very idea, that men illumined by the Divine Spirit should have deified a creature, and have led the whole Christian world into the grossest idolatry! Who but must tremble to conceive such horrible criminality in those faithful, unambitious followers of Jesus Christ? What could be their inducement to destroy all their own prospects of salvation, and involve in irremediable guilt, millions of their fellow-creatures? And upon the supposition that they neither believed this doctrine *themselves*, or intended to lead *others* into such a persuasion, what a wonderful coincidence of circumstances must it have been, to induce the effects which their writings have produced.

But if they believed themselves, what they have so fully taught (as every principle of candour and liberality, independent of higher motives, would lead us to conclude,) with what an accumulation of evidence is the GODHEAD of our blessed LORD confirmed and assured!

It were almost needless to add, concerning these apostles and first disciples of our Lord, "whose faith we ought to follow, considering the end of their conversation; Jesus Christ! the same yesterday, to-day, and for ever," (Heb. xiii. 7, 8.)

SERMON VIII.

MATTHEW XXII. 42.

What think ye of Christ?

If the importance of the subject to which I have of late so frequently requested your attention, did not supersede every other consideration, I should have thought it necessary to have prefaced several of the preceding discourses with an apology. But though I feel great apprehension, lest, from the very defective manner in which the subject hath been treated, I should have failed in my endeavours to exhibit the proofs of our Lord's GODHEAD in that strong point of view which may be requisite for the establishment of perfect conviction in your minds; (and which I cannot but think, would be the sure consequence arising from the evidences themselves, if taught of God;) yet I persuade myself that the humblest efforts in such an interesting cause, will need no recommendation with all sincere minds. To have a just and proper conception of *his* person and character, who is "the Author and Finisher of our faith," cannot but be desirable and gratifying to all his followers.

Nor is this the only object to be answered by it. The great question of our Lord's GODHEAD certainly involves the highest concerns of Christianity. Whoever wishes to derive comfort and assurance from the promises of the Gospel, and especially in the more interesting parts of it, which relate to the future prospects of our nature, must first be convinced of the truth of that authority on which the whole rests, that "He is faithful who has promised," (Heb. x. 23.) Neither do I conceive it possible that any man can experience the full extent of the consolations which the religion of Jesus affords, who hath not imbibed a portion of the same faith which actuated the apostle Paul: "I know (says he) whom I have believed, and I am persuaded that he is able to keep that which I have committed unto him against that day," (2 Tim. i. 12.)

But though the importance of the subject itself, may, I hope, in some degree, justify and account for the great length to which I have been necessarily led in the prosecution of it; yet it may be equally satisfactory now to observe, that with the present discourse I shall close it altogether, and relieve your attention. Having gone over the principal evidences of Scripture, and having omitted nothing material in the argument (as far as I can recollect), I desire to leave the final decision of the great question in the text, to every man's own mind in the sight of God: "What think ye of Christ?"

It was with this view, you may remember, that the several testimonies have been proposed for your consideration, in order that you might, in a free and unbiassed manner, draw such conclusions from them as, after mature deliberation and earnest prayer to God, should appear to you to be right and proper. Sensible of the weighty nature of the subject, it became a matter of conscience with me from the first, to be extremely cautious in advancing any thing in proof, but upon the most undeniable testimony. And as there appeared to be but one method by which this could be done, I have endeavoured to follow it, in making the Holy Scriptures the only standard of decision. If, however, I have in any point unknowingly departed from this rule, or if I have considered any of the sacred writers in a different sense from what they themselves intended, you will but behold in me a new instance of that very fallibility I have studied to avoid; and from this additional proof of human weakness or prejudice, and in the very exertion of what I may venture to name the sincerest and best intention, you will the more sensibly be convinced of the propriety of what I have suggested, that on subjects of this serious nature there should be no compulsion, but "let every man be fully persuaded (as the apostle speaks) in his own mind," (Rom. xiv. 5.)

Convinced, indeed, after all, from every observation of human nature, how apt the wisest are to err when left to the mere direction of their own minds, and that all our knowledge (more especially religious knowledge) must be derived from the teachings of the Divine Spirit (because that "no man can say that Jesus is the Lord, but by the Holy Ghost," 1 Cor. xii. 3,) I called upon you at our entrance upon the subject, to bend with me before the throne of God, and implore light and direction from heaven to precede our path, that the "Spirit of truth might guide us into all truth." And having now finished our researches, under an humble dependence on the divine aid, I must earnestly again request you to join with me in prayer, that our conclusions may be under the same gracious direction; "that in every thing being enriched by him, in all utterance, and in all knowledge, the testimony of Jesus may be confirmed in us, so that we come behind in no gift, waiting for the coming of our Lord Jesus Christ," (1 Corinth. i. 5, 6, 7.)

The intention of the present discourse is to take a brief survey of the several arguments which have been illustrated in a more copious manner, and by concentrating the whole evidence arising from thence, to shew the GODHEAD of Jesus in a more distinct and luminous point of view; it is on this account I therefore once more request your attention to the subject.

You will recollect, that the only object proposed from these Sermons, was an impartial and candid inquiry concerning the person and character of Jesus Christ. Whether he is to be classed among the frail and peccable race of men (as some professors of the Gospel have supposed,) or whether he is to be regarded in that sacred and exalted light (in which the established church of this country hath invariably considered him,) "as the eternal Son of God?"

In the investigation of this interesting question, my endeavours were first directed to shew that, from the appellation by which our blessed Lord is every where distinguished in the New Testament as the Son of God, there arose a strong presumptive evidence that his nature must be divine. For, when we find such a peculiar name uniformly marking his person; applied to him at the first by the angel which predicted his miraculous incarnation; afterwards confirmed by a supernatural voice from heaven, both at his baptism and at his transfiguration; assumed by Jesus himself, and particularly at a season the most critical, when it was made the pretence for his condemnation; that even spirits of darkness gave their testimony, however reluctantly, to the truth of it; and that this was the very name by which Christ was always known to his followers: it is hardly possible to conceive such a concurrence of circumstances in confirmation of our Lord's pretensions to this character, and yet that it should be a mere barren title without meaning. To a mind perfectly free from prejudice (as I then observed) the repeated and multifarious testimonies, which so fully and unequivocally distinguish our Lord by this term, must as decidedly prove his GODHEAD. For the phrase cannot, upon any ground, be applicable to him, but upon the clear assurance that he possessed an eternal existence with his Father underived from creation, by which he becomes truly and properly the Son of God.*

But as the mere name, unconnected with power, carries with it but the smallest degree of evidence to the GODHEAD of Jesus, I considered the argument arising

* Sermon I.

from hence but in a collateral point of view, and therefore passed on to circumstances more positive and substantial. In doing which I desired you to regard the great *criteria* of our Lord's divine nature, in the events which preceded his incarnation. The sacred writers have left upon everlasting record such accounts of Christ, and have ascribed to him such powers and operations, as when proved, cannot but impress the mind with the fullest conviction of his supreme dignity in whom those perfections are found.

In examining the testimonies of this kind, I then entered upon the proofs which we have in Scripture of our Lord's pre-existence, as the first circumstance which, in point of order, claimed our attention. And both from the words of Christ himself, as well as from the assurances of his apostles, I endeavoured to shew you, that no one fact can be more strongly attested, nor any truth more clearly proved, than that Christ had a state of existence antecedent to his incarnation.

The fact, however, of this superiority of nature, distinguishable in the person of Jesus, being supported by events still more palpable; the next observation to which our views were naturally directed, led us to consider Christ under those illustrious characters, which loudly proclaim his dignity; I mean as the Creator and Preserver of the universe. And as the clear conviction of this great truth became so highly important in the argument, I went very largely into this part of the subject, in gathering the evidences as they arise from Scripture, and brought before you the most unanswerable testimonies in proof of it. Such views of Christ being apparently conclusive in determining the certainty of his GODHEAD, a question involuntarily arises in the mind, how it is possible to resist such evidences? And surely, unless such evidences could wholly, or in a great measure, be refuted, there cannot be conceived any thing more daring than that of passing by all those testimonies of

Scripture, dethroning the Son of God, and bringing him down to the level of a poor peccable creature like ourselves! There should be, doubtless, some better ground to go upon than merely the airy conjectures and presumptuous reasonings of the human mind.

When I brought these proofs of Christ's GODHEAD before you, I desired you seriously to ponder the cogency of these solemn considerations. Whether any man can really suppose, that the meek and unaspiring temper of Jesus would have assumed divine honours, have declared his possession of "glory with his Father before the world," with other intimations of a similar nature, unless his claims were rightly founded? Or whether it is likely, that the servants of such a master should have been so forward in ascribing to him the incommunicable properties of the great Supreme, unless they had been most fully assured of the truth of what they asserted?*

Having proceeded thus far in the subject, in producing such proofs of our Lord's exalted character, as clearly justified the belief of his being more than human; I anticipated, and endeavoured to answer a question which appeared very likely to arise from hence; whether there are not discoverable some traces or appearances of Christ corresponding to these accounts, in the earlier ages of the world, and before his incarnation? For, though the facts which give belief to his divinity cannot be strengthened by any considerations of this kind (supposing the evidences themselves undeniable,) yet, if there can be discovered in the Old Testament any thing which shews a connexion with the account given of him in the New, it will serve no doubt to illustrate the point more fully, and altogether confirm our faith in the GODHEAD of Jesus.

Under this idea I requested you to examine with me

* Sermon II.

the Scriptures of the Old Testament, in order to learn what account we derive from thence concerning the person of our Lord. Though the subject, no doubt, is highly intricate, and enveloped in much mystery, yet I trust the reasons adduced were strong and satisfactory, to shew that there is great probability, that all the relations we meet with in these early ages of the world, of the appearance of a *personal* Jehovah, might, without violence to the sacred text, be considered as applicable to Jesus Christ. That every dispensation of the Father respecting mankind, has been uniformly carried on in the person of his blessed Son, that *he* is our Creator, our Preserver, our Reedemer, and finally will be our Judge. It will not be necessary for me to go over every evidence I then brought forward to substantiate my opinion, in order to awaken your remembrance. It will, I hope, answer every purpose to observe, that the circumstances I referred to were of such a nature and tendency, as made it difficult to account for them on a contrary persuasion.

Having discussed this difficult point, in the best manner I was able, I left it to your own reflections to make what inference you should think proper, and to determine whether a correspondence of circumstances so very striking (and strengthened at the same time by the previous view we had taken of our Lord's greatness of character, considered as the Creator and Preserver of the universe) did not amount to a certainty that Christ personally appeared in the world before his incarnation; and that all the dispensations of the Supreme Father respecting mankind have been conducted in the person of his divine Son.*

In our further pursuit of evidences, concerning the divinity of Jesus, it became a very natural and pertinent inquiry, to examine in the next place, what testimony or

* Sermon III.

account the prophets have given of this illustrious character. If those "holy men of old spake as they were moved by the Holy Ghost," (2 Pet. i. 21,) and professedly predicted the future events of the Messiah's kingdom, it certainly is an object highly expedient to our purpose, to know what they had declared of him. The inspiration under which they penned their prophetic writings must have preserved them from error; and the intention for which they wrote, makes it but reasonable to suppose, that in their accounts of the promised Messiah, they would sketch some of the more prominent features, at least, of his person and character.

With a view to the discovery of what those holy men had delivered, concerning Israel's Saviour, I again led your thoughts to the records of the Old Testament; and in order to investigate, as accurately as possible, the important question, I brought in review the predictions of all the prophets, which had written on the subject; I mean as far as related to our purpose. For as we were not seeking information concerning the *general* character of the Messiah, nor even the *particular* marks by which Jesus Christ proved himself to be the very person, I did not consider it needful to enumerate all the passages in the writings of the prophets, which had reference to the promised Saviour. The object of our inquiry was directed to a single point; namely, under what *character* was this Messiah to appear? Whether he was expected as *a divine being*, as mere *man*, or in a mysterious union of *both?*

In my endeavours to explore this point, agreeable to the plain and unperverted sense of the prophetic writings, I made many quotations from them, and the result was fairly and impartially stated. From the concurrent testimony of those venerable witnesses, it appeared evident that the great Deliverer of Israel, whom they predicted, was to come in the mysterious union of a great but humble Saviour; possessing divine attributes, by virtue of his eternal power and GODHEAD; and, at the same time, by means of the human nature, endowed with all the distinguishing properties of manhood. This was the character under which we found the prophets depicted the blessed Redeemer of the world.* And with this information we entered upon that era of the gospel, when Jesus Christ made his appearance in the flesh.

The events which signalized the life of Jesus were, in a very copious and extensive manner, made the subject of our next examination. From the moment of his miraculous birth, to his departure into heaven, in the view of his astonished disciples, you beheld how every incident tended to illustrate and confirm the truth of prophecy; that, while Christ appeared open to the full impressions of *humanity* in all its various departments, he manifested no less every evidence possible to prove his *divine nature*.

I endeavoured to conduct you through the several interesting particulars of this history of Jesus (at least such as had a more immediate reference to the great object of our inquiry;) and I hope that the effect which such views cannot but awaken in every true believer, is still strongly impressed upon your minds. Among these, I particularly recommended to your notice the evidences of our Lord's miraculous incarnation. And this being so very important an event in itself, and so satisfactory in proof of the subject we are upon, I dwelt the more largely upon it; and by adducing the several corroborating testimonies which confirm the fact; the prediction of prophecy, the information of the angel, the account of the sacred historian, and attested by the wonderful events which followed in the Redeemer's life, it should appear that no one circumstance can be more strongly certified and assured.

From the certain conviction of the wonderful birth

---

* Sermon IV.

of Jesus, I next proceeded to the evidences, equally demonstrable of the divine nature which appeared in his life. And first, of that astonishing series of miracles which he wrought. But as I then remarked to you, (and which I again particularly request may be duly observed,) it is not the miracles of Jesus simply considered in themselves, which proclaim his divinity; but it is the manner, the personal authority, by which they were performed, the forgiveness of sins, which sometimes accompanied them, and, above all, the ability Christ imparted to his disciples, of the same operations with himself: it is from these the inference of a superior and divine being, must be unavoidable. The evident line of distinction drawn between Jesus and all other workers of miracles, is such as one should expect to find between the actions of a lord and those of his servants. *They* wrought miracles to prove in whose authority they acted, *Jesus* to manifest his own.*

From the review of the miracles of our Lord, considered as testimonies of his divinity, my next proof of this doctrine was taken from the unparalleled discourses of Christ, which certainly carried with them a peculiar evidence to the same amount. In delivering his precepts to mankind, he taught (as was justly observed of him) "as one that had authority, and not as did the Scribes," (Matt. vii. 29.) The sublime topics of his religion; the awful purpose which he declared to be the great end of his coming; the language he assumed; the assurance he gave of raising the dead at the last day; the power he possessed, and said he would exert, of "drawing all men unto him," (John xii. 32;) in a word, the divine wisdom with which he taught, and the divine energy which accompanied his whole conversation, all highly demonstrate the unequalled excellence of our Lord's discourses, and utterly exclude the faintest gleam

---

* Sermon V.

of comparison between him and every other teacher. They prove indeed, "that never man spake as this man."

Proceeding in this methodical manner of examining the Scripture testimonies for the divinity of Jesus, my next step was, if possible, advancing yet higher in proof of it, in bringing the evidences, which declare him to have possessed all the attributes, and titles, and perfections of the Godhead. Every property known to be peculiar to the divine nature, you may recollect, was either very clearly to be distinguished in the person of our Lord, or ascribed to him by the sacred writers. To recapitulate those evidences which have been already so amply stated, would be superfluous and unnecessary. Let it suffice to say, that there is not an attribute or name, by which the incommunicable character of the great Jehovah is known in Scripture, but we find it equally applied to our blessed Lord, thereby explaining the sense of Christ's own words, when he said, "All things that the Father hath are mine," (John xvi. 15.) And surely it is highly incredible, that all the inspired writers should have thus concurred in describing the person of Jesus, under the terms by which the great Sovereign of the universe is known to his creatures, but upon the most absolute conviction that the facts are precisely as they have stated them.

The order which I observed in my arrangements of the evidences for Christ's divinity, led me next to mention *one* which I thought strongly tended to illustrate and prove the object in view: I mean the consideration of Jesus in that peculiar light which his religion represents him, as "the great sacrifice and oblation for sin." This cannot but imply a superiority in his nature equal to the object intended.

The miraculous incarnation of our Lord plainly intimated some important purpose, which could not be effected by a being merely human. And when we discover this purpose, as declared both by Christ and his apostles, was "to put away sin by the sacrifice of himself;" and behold the awful attestations which attended his last moments, all proclaiming that some grand design was wrought by his death, we cannot but feel an additional evidence arising from hence, of the divinity of his nature.

I trespass, I fear, in this recapitulation of the principal points in the several arguments which have been already noticed, but it is by this means only that they can be concentrated into one view. I shall be more brief, however, in the abstract of what remains. I would beg your recollection only of the concluding scenes of our Lord's ministry upon earth; his resurrection, his final commission to his disciples, his triumphal ascension into heaven, and his promised return as the Supreme Judge of quick and dead at the last day: such views of our Lord display a dignity in his character infinitely surpassing every idea of a being merely human. It is totally impossible to keep alive in our remembrance the persuasion of the simple humanity of Jesus, while we contemplate events of this superlative nature.

To behold him dismissing his few followers, and they of the lowest and most ignorant of the people, to the conversion of a world; assuring them of his constant presence and protection; breathing on them, and imparting the influence of the Holy Ghost; giving them power over unclean spirits, and for the working of all kinds of miracles; and having in a solemn and authoritative manner bestowed his benediction upon them; to see him carried up into heaven in the presence of his disciples: if such circumstances can be accounted for on common principles, or can be supposed possible, consistent with the nature of a mere *man;* then ought they not to be regarded as evidences of any thing *superior* in our blessed Lord; but if they are absolutely unparalleled, and altogether incompatible, except on the presumption of divinity, I cannot perceive how the inference which necessarily results from them can be avoided, that Jesus is "the Son of God."

And when we take into the account the great scene which is to close our Lord's ministry, in the supreme office he will exercise at the last day, as the Judge of men; when he is to come, "attended with an innumerable train of angels," and in a state of glory, surpassing all conception: at whose coming, "all that are in their graves shall hear his voice," and before "whose presence heaven and earth shall flee away:" I have no idea how the sacred writers could have described to mankind the appearance of Jehovah, in a manner more completely sublime and magnificent!

But surely, such accounts can never correspond with the notion that all this refers but to the coming of an human being! Is it likely that the grave should give up the dead at the voice of a man? that angels should attend his train, and even heaven and earth pass away at his presence? Nay more, that a mere glorified man should be appointed to be the supreme Arbiter of the everlasting fate of millions, or that he should be qualified for such acts as to read the heart, and know the exact motive of every single action; to ascertain real from unintentional guilt, and to determine, with perfect justice, the several portions of reward or punishment due to every individual? Besides, (as I remarked to you) what reason can be found for the elevation of a man to a station so astonishingly high, and without all parallel? Whereas, upon the supposition of our Lord's divine nature, every difficulty vanishes, and the whole dispensation of the gospel, relating to the person and character of its blessed Author, is probable, just, and uniform, and what our pure and uncorrupt notions of things might have conceived. He who made the world, and by whose power it is preserved, assumes a body of flesh to redeem it; and having, by this mysterious process, accomplished the purpose intended, he returns to his original state of glory, until he comes at the last day to judgment. Thus all the executive parts of the divine government are begun and carried on, and will be completed by *him,* who is the same "yesterday, to-day, and for ever."*

Having thus reviewed, in the relation of Scripture, and the events of our Saviour's life, the various testimonies to his divinity, I then closed the examination of evidences, in endeavouring to ascertain what was the opinion of those artless and undesigning servants of Christ, his apostles, upon the subject; and when their sentiments are added to the general account, I trust the whole, taken together, will be found forming a body of evidence little short of demonstration. With so solid and impregnable a chain of proofs (to use the language of one of old) is this great doctrine of the Christian church bound up and fortified.

I have now, in as regular and progressive an order as the nature of the subject would admit, gone over the evidences of Scripture concerning the GODHEAD of CHRIST: and I have endeavoured to perform this duty in the plainest and most impartial manner possible; not by a long train of arguments addressed to men of science only, but in a form of words adapted to every comprehension, that like the prophet's vision, "he which runs may read," (Habak. ii. 2.) Whether I have been sufficiently successful in the proofs adduced to satisfy every candid mind, I know not; yet I venture to believe some light hath been thrown upon the subject to guide the serious in their inquiry after the truth, respecting this great article of faith.

You have seen that the testimonies in favour of this opinion are strong and numerous, and such as do not depend upon one or two passages in the word of God,

* Sermon VI.

of a doubtful meaning, expressed in parable or figure, but of the clearest construction, and in terms liable to no ambiguity. It is incredible, therefore, to suppose, that so many and various circumstances should concur to induce the belief of a doctrine which is altogether unauthorized and ill-founded! If this faith was derived from an oblique intimation, cursorily delivered by any of the sacred writers, and at a time when the merit of the great Redeemer's character was the topic of discourse; if it depended upon the opinion of a single apostle, or if it were noticed but in one part of Scripture; or if the thing itself was totally repugnant to all reason and common sense: in either of these cases there might be some plausibility of argument for refusing, or at least suspending, our opinion upon a matter of this consequence; and we should be justified in demanding some higher proofs, before we subscribed to this part of our creed. But when we behold the thing itself, connected by a chain of testimony running through the whole volume of Scripture; and such perfections, and attributes, and characters, as are utterly incompatible, except with GODHEAD, possessed by our blessed Lord, and without all scruple applied to him by every one of the inspired writers: when proofs of this kind all concentrate in the person of Jesus, to certify his divine nature; ought it not to be some mighty argument to counterbalance such powerful evidences, and not a few detached phrases of Scripture delivered in a desultory way, and such, perhaps, as if properly considered and explained, with reference to the occasion, the time, the place, or persons to whom they were addressed, would be found not unfavourable to the doctrine.

But you are to determine for yourselves under GOD's grace, what degree of respect is due to the evidences which you have now reviewed. And let me hope that this determination will not be made from the hasty impulse of the moment, but rather be the serious result of a proper deliberation, and humble waiting in prayer upon the LORD. " I speak as to wise men, judge ye what I say," (1 Corinth. x. 15.) Remember, it is not a mere point of speculation or curiosity which teacheth no further than the opinion; but it is an object which includes in its consequences all the great hopes of human nature. I have already more than once observed, and now finally wish to leave the full force of the observation upon your minds, that, together with the GODHEAD of CHRIST, must stand or fall, all the peculiar and momentous doctrines of his gospel. Every thing interesting in Christianity is founded on the greatness of the Author's character. Even the *moral* precepts of his religion lose much of their dignity, and their authority is debased, if the founder be not more than man: nor hath the New Testament any thing higher to recommend it, except in novelty, than the legation of Moses.

If this be the real state of things, and the Christian's Lord be not divine, farewell to all the hopes of the faithful: his consolations are no more! Then all the gracious promises of religion, so highly encouraging to repentance and amendment of life, and with which the anxious mind, when smitten with a sense of guilt, sought a requiem, are done away, and the law of God, strict and unalterable in its demands, stands forth before the guilty conscience, arrayed in all its terrors. To what refuge shall the awakened sinner now fly, or in what sacrifice can he again place confidence? I thought (he will say) my soul secure in the expectation of pardon for my sins, through the meritorious death of God my Saviour. I understood that the apostles of Christ had instructed the world in this doctrine, that God " was in Christ, reconciling the world unto himself, not imputing their trespasses unto them," (Matt. xx. 28;) but if this be all a delusion, I am robbed of my best comforts, and am without hope. Tell me not of the virtues of human nature; for how shall any man build his hopes of acceptance with his Maker, upon the sandy foundation of the purity of his own life! Alas! my very best deeds are largely tinctured with a mixture of infirmity. I see a mark of imperfection strongly appearing in every page of my life. And for the errors and intentional sins of nature, " should the Lord be extreme to mark all that is done amiss, who may abide it?" (Psalm cxxx. 3.) How then " by the deeds of the law shall any flesh be justified?" (Rom. iii. 20.)

And what is repentance? a patched up, blemished, and imperfect repentance, made up of alternate sorrow and sin? To-day feeling the compunction of guilt; to-morrow falling again perhaps into the same or similar transgressions: the next day renewing the serious impression, and soon after giving fresh proofs of human infirmity: and thus going on through life in the succession of offences and contrition; sometimes humbling the soul under the mighty hand of God, from a conscious unworthiness, but more frequently forgetting that " there is a God which judgeth the earth." Are these sacrifices fit to offer to the Lord? Are these fragments of a chequered life sufficiently meritorious to save the soul? Can any man be presumptuous enough to satisfy his mind that heaven *must be* the *reward* of such a train of conduct?

Considering the miserable consequence to which the rejection of our Lord's divine nature necessarily leads, and the despondency it creates in the human mind; one should imagine that the advocates for this doctrine, however secretly convinced that they are *right*, must yet wish to be *wrong:* for, surely it is the most comfortless doctrine ever proposed to mankind! To consider ourselves in a fallen, helpless state of being, exposed to various dangers, and surrounded with the numerous temptations which beset the path of duty, and in this situation to have no divine Spirit to look up to, as the helper of our infirmities, nor any divine Redeemer to confide in, as the propitiation of our sins: conscious also of being accountable creatures, and that a day is approaching when all our actions will be brought into judgment, with every secret thought, whether it be good or bad: can there be a more discouraging and comfortless religion than this? And especially when the retrospect of life is clouded over, I do not say barely with frailties, but with *wilful* offences. To have no better support than repentance, and no refuge but what arises from the uncovenanted mercy of God: ignorant at the same time, whether *that* repentance hath been exercised in due proportion to our sins, or whether that *mercy* will be extended equal to our necessities. However hopes of this kind may sooth the mind with the speciousness of their promises, when that mind is perfectly at ease, and the awful subjects of futurity are considered as at a distance; yet when a man is just closing the book of life, and hovering between this world and the next, then it is to be apprehended, mere abstract arguments will entirely lose their efficacy. And indeed, if experience can be deemed the truest test for the ascertaining a matter of fact, we have every reason to conclude, that *those* leave the world with most complacency and satisfaction, who have learned to place their hopes and confidence in a *Saviour's merit*, and not in *their own*.

But it may be said, that we are not to judge of a doctrine by its consequences, as they may appear to us. Truth must ultimately prevail, and our duty is to anticipate her decisions. Be this, then, the great object of pursuit. Examine with all possible care and circumspection the testimonies for the GODHEAD of Jesus, which have been now proposed to your consideration, and be guided in your opinion, as you would upon any other important concern of life. Where the evidences are most palpable and convincing, there let the decision of the point rest. Ask your own heart, whether it be possible to imagine that such an accumulation of proofs as you have now seen, uniting in testimony to this great truth, should conspire in support of any cause, unless the probability were in its favour. And do not wonder that this great object of faith is not entirely free from every difficulty: rather wonder that in so mysterious a dispensation as the recovery of a lost world, and by means so astonishing, matters should be so much understood by us as they really are: that such a creature as man, who is but just crept into being, should be able to look round about him, and behold even the surface of the *deep things of God.*

But whatever your conclusions may be, may divine grace confirm and strengthen the faith of all who are in the *right*, and mercifully bring into the way of truth every one of his people who is in error. The hour is hastening fast upon us, when we shall be exercised no more with the mysteries of religion, nor will the blessed Redeemer of the world be any longer the object of our faith, but "we shall see him as he is, and know even as we are known." God grant that in that awful hour, our faith in his sight may not be reproved; but that it may then appear we have given, during the present day of trial, an earnestness of attention to the great demands of duty suitable to their importance, and have diligently set our hearts to a serious concern for the one thing needful. And oh! that God may daily assist every humble soul, that does this more and more with his grace. And "may the Lord direct your hearts into the love of God, and into the patient waiting for Jesus Christ," (1 Thess. iii. 5.)

But for you, who live in the faith of this persuasion (and I trust I speak to numbers of that description,) I must not dismiss the consideration of this important subject without observing, in what a serious and awful manner the perfect conviction of this great truth ought to affect our hearts. Satisfied as we are by a series of proofs, the most full and incontestible, that the gracious scheme of salvation contained in the gospel was proposed to mankind by no less a being than the Son of God himself: think, I beseech you, with what increased veneration and regard, *we*, above all men, ought to receive this "glorious gospel of the blessed God," (1 Tim. i. 11.) Is then the great Author of our religion really and truly the Son of God? Did he possess "glory with his Father before the world?" And was there no other method in all the plans of Omnipotence for the recovery of our fallen nature, but for this divine character to come down from heaven, to enshrine his glory in a veil of flesh, and by a process the most painful and humiliating, to procure the means of our salvation and happiness? Was there no less being, no angel, equal to the accomplishment of it? Dread Lord! what awful and awakening views ought it to excite in our minds of the importance of that scheme of grace and mercy which he brought; and with what earnestness ought our souls to be engaged in seeking wisdom from above, lest any man fail of this grace of God. Surely, the higher ideas we entertain of the great Author of our faith, the higher must arise in proportion, the duty and obedience we owe him. Let those professors of Christianity who consider Jesus but as a *man*, regard but as the ministry of a *man*, all the interesting doctrines of his religion. For the whole of his gospel being enervated by this persuasion, they cannot, they ought not, indeed, to feel it in the manner it should affect us. But we who, in the person of Jesus, behold the eternal GOD one with the Father; by this consideration, how exceedingly enforced upon the conscience are all the sanctions of the divine laws! Let it not, therefore, for shame, be ever said, that either in affection or in duty *their* conduct is equal to *ours*; but let us shew the superiority of our faith by a corresponding practice; and let the remembrance of that just and awakening consideration of the apostle's be never from our hearts, how "impossible it will be in the end for any of us to escape, if we neglect so great salvation."

Particularly, let the awful view of the sad nature of guilt be one of those principles most deeply impressed upon the mind, in the consciousness of the divinity of the great Author of our religion.

Never was there afforded an event equally demonstrable of the dreadful malignity of sin, as when Christ became man, to redeem the world from its influence. The promulgation of the law on mount Sinai, though accompanied with such manifestations of the divine presence, was by no means so strong an indication of the value of righteousness in the sight of God, as when his divine Son appeared in an human form to proclaim it to the world. And of all arguments which can be thought of to interest the human heart to resist the contagion of sin, and to stimulate to purity of life and manners, no doubt that is infinitely transcendant which is drawn from the incarnation, and sufferings, and death of Jesus.

Let the solemn conviction, then, of the great malignity of sin be always connected in our remembrance with the assurance of *his* divine nature, who came to expiate its effects: and if "God is of purer eyes than to behold iniquity," (Habak. i. 13;) if "no evil can possibly dwell with him," (Psalm v. 4;) if he hath given so decided a proof of his utter detestation of sin, as even "to send his Son to be the Saviour of the world," (1 John iv. 14:) What shall I say? If the redemption of sinners could only be effected by means so awful and extraordinary; *shall we* dare to *continue in sin,* after such a manifestation of the divine displeasure against it? "Shall we," who are supposed by virtue of the death of Jesus, to be ourselves "dead unto sin, live any longer therein, (Rom. vi. 12:) God forbid. We are now bought with a price, and are no longer our own;" and therefore we are bound by a peculiar obligation to holiness, and "to glorify God in our body, and in our spirit, which are God's," (1 Cor. vi. 20.) In a word, *we* who receive the doctrine of a divine Being in our Redeemer, are justly expected, above all others, "to be examples of believers, in word, in conversation, in charity, in spirit, in faith, and purity," (1 Tim. iv. 12.)

And these duties, let us further remember, are enforced upon us by considerations, if possible, yet more importunate. Every additional proof of God's love must proportionably increase the apprehension of his anger. Every abused mercy is converted into an evil. And what is intended for our happiness, by a misapplication or neglect, must become the source of misery. "If we sin wilfully after we have received the knowledge of the truth, there remaineth no more sacrifice for sins, but a certain fearful looking for of judgment, and fiery indignation which shall devour the adversaries," (Heb. x. 26, 27.) How ought our souls to be impressed with the conviction of these undoubted truths! For, depend upon it, of all condemnation which may fall upon the sinner at the last day, that Christian's must be the heaviest and most intolerable, who, with the open profession and belief of the divinity of Jesus, hath lived a wicked and disobedient life. "Far better would it have been never to have known the way of righteousness, than after having known, to turn from the holy commandment delivered unto us," (2 Pet. ii. 21.) And if the righteous scarcely are saved, where shall the ungodly and the sinner appear?" (1 Pet. iv. 18.)

From the accumulation of evidences with which this great doctrine of the GODHEAD of Christ hath been now proved, I hope no sincere believer in the divinity of his Lord, entertains the least apprehension, as though "that faith" is in any danger of being overthrown, "which was once delivered to the saints," (Jude 3.) That gracious Providence which watched over and guarded it, while a tender plant, from every storm, will not suffer it now (to use our Lord's own beautiful figure,) when it has waxed a great tree, and its branches have filled the earth, to be cut down and destroyed. By feeble instruments was it first planted, and, under divine protection, the same humble means will in all ages be found sufficient for its security and support.

When the fashionable doctrine of the present hour has had its day, like many others which have sprung up, and for the moment appeared to flourish, but soon died away, "whose very memorial is perished with them," (Psalm ix. 6;) this also will sink and be forgotten. And as the false god could not stand before the ark of the Lord, though repeatedly set in his place, but fell upon his face to the earth, (1 Sam. v. 3, 4;) so this, and all other deviations from the true faith, must ultimately bend to the doctrine of the divinity of Jesus; the "true God (as John calls him) and eternal life," (1 John v. 20.)*

---

* As I am now about to take leave of my reader, I would request the favour of him, before our final separation, that he would pause one moment, and ask himself this necessary question? What kind of conviction the evidences which have been now brought before him, in proof of the GODHEAD of Jesus, are likely to leave upon his mind? There is a conviction of the *head*, and which there is great reason to fear, by what appears in the world, is but too common, with which men satisfy their minds on this great subject of the Redeemer's divinity: and this is certainly very attainable by the mere dint of reasoning, and men of no real religion may possess it. But then this is a loose, floating, undetermined principle of belief, which descends not into the *heart*, and neither interests the affections nor influences the conduct, and is productive of no one practical effect on the life. Should your conviction of Christ's GODHEAD, my brother, after all that I have brought before you, operate to no higher purpose than this; forgive me if I add, that according to my ideas your belief, or disbelief, of the important doctrine, is much the same.

When I read the writings of learned and ingenious men, which have been published in proof of the GODHEAD of the Lord Jesus Christ; and see how much may be said, from the mere strength of human reasoning alone, on this divine subject, I very heartily subscribe to the just compliment their labours are entitled to, and add my thanks to the general sufferage of mankind, for their services in defence of the common faith. But after paying all possible respect to the attainments of human learning, I confess that I derive more real, solid satisfaction from the single

But O, what topics of persuasion shall I adopt, so as to leave a lasting impression of these truths upon every

---

experimental testimony of some poor unlettered Christian, whom God hath taught on this grand point, than from all the elaborate discourses of the most learned of men. The *one* may, indeed, and will gratify the understanding by the elegance of style, or the manner of the remarks, but the *other*, however plain and unpolished, comes with what the apostle calls "the demonstration of the Spirit and power," and is as much superior to mere abstract reasoning and argument as any ocular proof surpasses the best hearsay evidence whatever. Would you covet, my Christian friend, the possession of this gratifying conviction? seek it then of Him, "from whom alone cometh every good and every perfect gift." Outward evidences you may obtain from the hearing of the ear. Inward testimony is not to be found in books. But every one, the apostle says, "who believeth on the Son of God," that is, who believeth to any effectual purpose of salvation, "hath the witness in himself." Grant, Lord, this witness to all thy people, "that our faith may not stand in the wisdom of men, but in the power of God!" (1 Cor. ii. 5.)

Might I venture to go one step further in the observation, I would say, that according to my apprehension of things, not only this fundamental truth in the Christian system, the Divinity of Christ, but every other article of the holy faith connected with it, is capable, through the gracious teachings of God, of being brought home to the conviction of the mind, with evidences so perfectly clear and irresistible, as to leave no manner of doubt of their existence and reality. Indeed, might I escape the imputation of vanity upon this occasion, (which when it be considered how utterly repugnant every degree of it is to the principles of the Gospel, methinks one might be credited in saying, it is my most earnest wish studiously to avoid,) I would, as modestly as the case will admit of, venture to assert, that there is not an essential article in the creed of a real Christian, but what I can experimentally subscribe to, and have received as ample conviction of, as I think could have been received by the demonstration of sight. Suffer me to explain myself by an illustration. For example. The resurrection and ascension of Jesus, forms a principal doctrine in the faith of a Christian. Now I humbly conceive, that I have the most heartfelt and satisfactory conviction of the certainty of the resurrection and ascension of Jesus, equal to any evidence whatever which could be afforded. And I thus prove it. Before the sufferings and death of Jesus, he told his disciples of the necessity of his going from them, and the consequences which should result from his departure. "It is expedient for you (says Christ) that I go away: for if I go not away the Comforter will not come unto you: but if I depart I will send him unto you. And when he is come, he will reprove the world of sin, and of righteousness, and of judgment," (John xvi. 7, 8.) Hence, therefore, I prove the certainty of the resurrection and ascension of Jesus, from the certainty of those effects which have followed, agreeably to his promises. And I must insist upon it, with all the confidence of one that contends for a plain matter of fact, that from the very mo-

mind, to be the perpetual incentive of all our conduct? I will say with the apostle, " But ye, beloved, building

ment that the Holy Ghost first descended on the day of Pentecost, to the present hour, in every single instance where the operations of the blessed Spirit have been experienced on the minds of believers; in that breast the Lord hath given as complete an evidence of the resurrection and ascension of Jesus, as to any of those " to whom he shewed himself alive after his passion by many infallible proofs:" and, " who stedfastly looked toward heaven " in his ascension" as he went up, (Acts i. 3, 10.)

And if it will not be considered going out of my way to remark, I would add yet further, the certainty of the doctrine of the Holy Trinity may be proved also by the same infallible evidences, to the comfort of all gracious minds, who will but attend to the operations in their own hearts of the Three sacred and eternal Persons of the Godhead. For when Jesus says, " No man can come to me except the Father which hath sent me draw him;" and the believer finds himself drawn to Christ with an earnestness and a persuasion which nothing else can satisfy, that Christ is all-sufficient to his salvation; can any thing be more decisive in proof, both of the existence and of the operations of the Father? And again, when a soul, conscious of being by nature " dead in trespasses and sins," finds himself quickened by grace to a new and spiritual life; and reads in Scripture, among numberless other proofs of the divinity and power of Jesus, that " as the Father raiseth up the dead and quickeneth them, even so the Son quickeneth whom he will," (John v. 21;) will not the soul thus quickened, be able to discern the clear traces of the Redeemer's eternal power and Godhead in this distinguished act of grace? And so, in like manner, to that awakened Christian, " in whose heart the love of God is shed abroad by the Holy Ghost," when he is conscious that before this, the enmity of a carnal nature remained; will higher proof be required of the divinity and operation of the blessed Spirit than his own experience thus affords him? These evidences (and numberless others, which, if needful, might be produced,) are what I call practical and experimental proofs of the doctrine of the Holy Trinity, and which if real Christians would but attend to in their own experience, they would be found more than sufficient, both to check the blasphemous tongue of heresy, and " to quench all the fiery darts of the wicked."

My Christian brother! I add no more, but an earnest prayer to God, that instead of turning over the many volumes of human arguments which have been written for and against these divine things, (which unless blessed with an higher Teacher than man, leave the world just where they found it;) that you would turn over the volume of your own life, and see what pages there are marked with the teachings of God's Holy Spirit. May God teach you the certainty of the Redeemer's divinity, by that most decisive of all evidences, his grace in your heart; for then you will be able to adopt similar language to what the men of Samaria did to the woman at the well: " Now we believe, (say they) not because of thy saying, for we have heard him ourselves, and know that this is indeed the Christ, the Saviour of the world," (John iv. 42.)

up yourselves on your most holy faith, praying in the Holy Ghost, keep yourselves in the love of God, looking for the mercy of our Lord Jesus Christ unto eternal life," (Jude 20, 21.) And let the expectation of this *eternal life* excite our daily preparation for it. Let the employments of our *future* state become our principal subject of contemplation in the *present*. Let every hour be such as we would wish our last to be. And when the scene of this life is drawing to its end, and the hand of death is closing our mortal eyes for ever, may the last faint accents which tremble on our lips, be in unison with the beginning of our everlasting song: "Salvation to our God which sitteth upon the throne, and unto the Lamb. Blessing, and glory, and wisdom, and thanksgiving, and honour, and power, and might, be unto our God, for ever and ever," Amen, (Rev. vii. 10, 12.)